A PLUME BOOK

THE DORD, THE DIGLOT,
AND AN AVOCADO OR TWO

ANU GARG is the founder of Wordsmith.org, a community of word lovers throughout the world, in two hundred countries. He is the author of two bestsellers on the joy of words. He lives in the Seattle area with his wife and daughter.

The Dord, the Diglot,

and an

Avocado or Two

~

*The Hidden Lives and
Strange Origins of Words*

~

ANU GARG

A PLUME BOOK

PLUME
Published by Penguin Group
Penguin Group (USA) Inc., 375 Hudson Street, New York, New York 10014,
U.S.A. • Penguin Group (Canada), 90 Eglinton Avenue East, Suite 700,
Toronto, Ontario, Canada M4P 2Y3 (a division of Pearson Penguin Canada Inc.)
• Penguin Books Ltd., 80 Strand, London WC2R 0RL, England • Penguin Ire-
land, 25 St. Stephen's Green, Dublin 2, Ireland (a division of Penguin Books
Ltd.) • Penguin Group (Australia), 250 Camberwell Road, Camberwell, Victo-
ria 3124, Australia (a division of Pearson Australia Group Pty. Ltd.) • Penguin
Books India Pvt. Ltd., 11 Community Centre, Panchsheel Park, New Delhi – 110
017, India • Penguin Group (NZ), 67 Apollo Drive, Rosedale, North Shore 0745,
Auckland, New Zealand (a division of Pearson New Zealand Ltd.) • Penguin
Books (South Africa) (Pty.) Ltd., 24 Sturdee Avenue, Rosebank, Johannesburg
2196, South Africa

Penguin Books Ltd., Registered Offices: 80 Strand, London WC2R 0RL, England

First published by Plume, a member of Penguin Group (USA) Inc.

First Printing, November 2007
10 9 8 7 6 5 4 3 2

Ⓟ REGISTERED TRADEMARK—MARCA REGISTRADA

LIBRARY OF CONGRESS CATALOGING-IN-PUBLICATION DATA
Garg, Anu.
    The dord, the diglot, and an avocado or two : the hidden lives and strange ori-
gins of words / Anu Garg.
        p. cm.
    ISBN 978-0-452-28861-4 (trade pbk.)
    1. English language—Etymology.   I. Title.
    PE1574.G27 2007
    422—dc22

                                                                    2007006583

Printed in the United States of America
Set in Goudy
Designed by Eve L. Kirch

Compared to the drama of words, Hamlet is a light farce.
—Anatoly Liberman

Contents

Introduction

What are words? The raw material for poetry, novels, plays, stories, and epics. But words are stories in themselves—each word has a story.

If you were looking for a book with the largest collection of stories in the world—all true stories—you wouldn't have to look far. You probably already have that book: a dictionary. No wonder the French novelist Anatole France called a dictionary "the universe in alphabetical order." This book is a collection of some of the more interesting stories behind words.

Each word has a biography. It tells us about its parents, where it was born, which corners of the world it traveled, and what twists and turns it took to reach where it is today. That biography of a word—the story behind it—is called etymology (from Greek *etymos*: true).

The parentage of some words remains obscure, waiting for a few intrepid detectives to trace, unearth, dig out, and explain. That doesn't stop speculators, though. For example, there are dozens of stories, each appearing to be the real one, for the origin of the term *eighty-six* (to discard, to refuse, or to be out of something).

Can you see a tooth in a dandelion? That's how we got the word *dandelion*. It came to English from the French language.

In French, *dent-de-lion* means "tooth of a lion"—because its leaves look like the sharp teeth of a fearsome lion.

Even the words for the most mundane things have unusual stories. What do a bicycle and a biscuit have in common? Both begin with the letters *b-i*. *Bi* means two. So a bicycle has two wheels. And a biscuit is twice baked (or, at least, they used to be).

The little tags at the ends of shoelaces are called aglets. That's because in French, *aiguille* means "needle" and *aiguillette* is a "little needle." So an aglet makes a shoelace work like a needle that we can thread through the holes in our shoes. Those holes are called eyelets, or "little eyes."

A chad is the little circle that's cut out when you punch a hole in a sheet of paper. Why is it called a chad? Nobody knows. Sometimes the origin of a word is a mystery yet to be solved.

This book is a collection of stories behind words. It is not meant to be a comprehensive treatise on the origins of words; rather, it presents a selection of some of the most fascinating stories behind words.

The Dord, the Diglot,

and an

Avocado or Two

~ *Chapter 1* ~

Hidden Lives of Everyday Words

We often believe movie actors have fascinating lives. We crave to know about the childhoods of rock stars. Popular magazines dish out scoops on celebrities, because, after all, who wants to know about the life of the everyman on the street?

Yet if we get to know even the most ordinary-looking persons on the street, we'll learn that they have fascinating stories to tell. Each man's and woman's life could be an opera, if only we took the time to discover more about them—where they were born, what they did while growing up, what makes them tick, what their dreams and wishes are, and more.

The same goes with words. Sure, "celebrity" words have charming stories to tell (the word *googol*, coined by a nine-year-old boy, became the inspiration behind the naming of the Google search engine), but rank-and-file words in a dictionary have had lives that are intriguing, too. Their origins involve lovely stories as well. Here are a few of them.

PUPIL

The two senses of this word—a student and the part in the center of the eye—are related. We got this word from the Latin *pupus* meaning "a boy" and *pupa* meaning "a girl." Remember the pupa of a butterfly? It's the same word.

Now what about the part in the center of the eye through which light enters? Have you seen your reflection in someone's eyes? How tiny it appears! Even adults appear small like little children in other people's eyes. And that's why that part of the eye is called a pupil.

DIPLOMA

A diploma is a paper we get from a school when we complete a course. But why is that paper called a diploma? It's because traditionally that paper was folded in two, and the Greek word *diplo* means "double" or "in pairs"; these days doctors and dentists proudly display their diplomas not folded but framed on their waiting room walls.

The word *diplomat* is related. Long ago, *diplomatic* meant "relating to documents." The shift in the sense occurred from the titles of collections of documents that were related to international relations. So *diplomatic corps* shifted in meaning from a body of documents to a diplomatic cadre in a nation's capital.

There's a dinosaur with a name starting with *diplo*: diplodocus. That's because it has two long parts: a long neck and a long tail.

BLESS

When we bless someone, we wish for their well-being. We want the best for them, and the last thing we'd think about is for them to be bloodied, but that's the origin of the word. That hidden blood becomes visible in the Old English form of the word: *bledsian*. Consecrating something involved smearing sacrificial blood over it.

In French, the word *blesser* still means "to wound." So if you go to France and they say you are *blessable*, watch out. They are not saying you are suitable for blessing, rather you are susceptible to being wounded.

ADMIRAL

What could the commander in chief of a fleet have in common with a Muslim ruler? Well, they are one and the same thing, etymologically speaking. Admiral is another form of the word *emir/amir*, the title of the head of state in some Islamic countries. It came from *amir al* meaning "commander of."

SYMPOSIUM

While in graduate school I took part in many symposia and seminars on topics related to my field of study: computer science. If only I'd known the hidden meanings of those words at the time. . . . *Symposium* was originally a drinking party, and *seminar* came from "semen." No wonder so many students go to college.

Drinking has a way of relaxing the tongue, and that idea grew into the current sense of symposium—where people gather to engage in conversation on a topic. *Seminar* came from "semen" via "seminary." *Semen* is Latin for "seed," and in earlier times a seminary was a place where students were developed and cultivated. It was a place for learning anything, not necessarily theology.

LADY

A *lady* was, literally, a loaf kneader, from Old English *hlaf* (loaf) + *dige* (kneader). A *lord*, in turn, was a loaf guard. Well,

1. What Russian author adopted a pen name that meant "most poison"?

we've come a long way from those olden times. Today a lady may well be commanding a spacecraft instead of kneading a loaf of bread. A lord may be pushing a baby stroller instead of guarding the loaf (though, idiomatically speaking, lords are supposed to be responsible for their bun in the oven till it comes out—and for many years afterward.)

What is a *woman*? She is a female human being, from Old English *wif-man*, from *wife* (female) + *man* (human being). Earlier the word *man* was used to describe anyone of the human race. *Wife* was the term for a female, not necessarily the spouse of someone.

DESSERT

You've enjoyed your dinner, plates have been removed from the table, and now you're ready for dessert. That setting alludes to the origin of the word *dessert*. The word came from the French *desservir*, meaning "to clear the table." That's because dessert is often served after the table has been cleared. *Dessert: de + serve*.

Desert is from Latin *deserere* (to abandon). On the other hand, *desert* in the expression *just deserts* means "deserved"— it's from a little-known word *desert* (deserving), from Old French *deservir* (to de serve). So *just deserts* indicates something justly deserved or merited.

TAXICAB

A *taxi* is, well, one which taxes. It's a shortened form of *taximeter*, which is the name of the device that calculates the fare. And *cab* is short for *cabriolet*. A cabriolet was originally a

> *2.* Which country has the largest number of English speakers in the world? Hint: It's neither in Europe nor in the Americas.

two-wheeled, one-horse carriage, so called because of its light movement. You could say it capered since it's derived from the Latin root *capr-* (goat), which also gave us *Capricorn*. From goat to a one-horse carriage to a modern taxi, it has been a long journey.

WINDOW

Now here's an etymology that speaks of the poetry of words. A *window* is, literally, the "wind's eye." Look at how a window opens to let the wind in, and it'll be clear why it was so named in Old Norse, from which it moved into English.

INSPIRATION

When we are inspired, the breath of life has been blown into us because that's where the word came from: Latin *spirare* (to breathe). And it's easy to see what happens when we stop breathing: we expire.

A similar word—*afflatus*—takes life from the same idea, that one is inspired. It's derived from Latin *flare* (to blow), which also gave us *flatulence*.

STATIONERY

If you can't remember when to use the spelling *stationary* and when *stationery*, take comfort in the fact that both words are the same, or used to be.

Stationers sell stationery—writing material—and they were called that because they were stationary, they had permanent shops, as opposed to peddlers, who moved from place to place.

TRAVEL

The word *travel* comes from another word, *travail*, which means hard, painful work. Imagine for a moment, you're living in a time five hundred years ago. There are no cars with comfy seats, no airplanes to take you anywhere in the world within hours. You have to travel on a horse, or in a wagon, for days or even months. The road is bumpy and there are no roadside McFriendly's restaurants.

Travel was truly hard work.

JEOPARDY

Earlier, jeopardy was a game with an even chance, from Old French *jeu* (game) and *parti* (divided). Today the odds have gone down for the word *jeopardy*. Someone in jeopardy could be facing something truly hazardous to life—risk of harm or death. The word *hazard* is from Arabic *al-zahr* (the die). Those dice can be hazardous, especially in Las Vegas.

EASEL

Vana go painting? Climb on an equus asinus. We can thank the Dutch for this crass name for an artist's frame to support a canvas. They thought it looked like an ass, which in the Dutch language is *ezel*, and named it accordingly.

JARGON

In Old French, *jargon* was the chattering of birds. But then again, listen to a bunch of economists or doctors or engineers talk, and it would seem maybe the word still means the same.

SALARY

We hope you can buy more than just salt with your salary, but at one time that's what *salary* was for. The word *salary* came to English from the Latin *salarium*, which means an allowance for salt. In olden times salt was expensive. So soldiers used to get rations of salt. The word came from the Latin *sal*, meaning "salt." The word *salad* is related, because in the old days a *salad* was usually *salted*.

ETIQUETTE

Did you notice that the word *ticket* and *etiquette* have similar sounds? That's because both words have the same French origin. In olden times visitors to French courts were given a book that listed court ceremonies. It also told the visitors how to behave during those ceremonies. You can think of that book as a ticket to the court. Today, having proper etiquette can be one's ticket to good company.

POLITE

When you're polite, you're polished, from Latin *polire* (to polish). Don't we all love someone who's polished rather than one who's rough? When we are polished our rough edges are taken away and we are smooth and well rounded.

GLAMOUR

Believe it or not, this word is another form of the word *grammar*. The magical charm sense of the word arose because *grammar*, or learning, used to be associated with the occult.

I think we have an opportunity here. If only all those glamour magazines had a section on grammar, we wouldn't have to worry anymore about the state of language proficiency in the world.

PLAGIARISM

When one plagiarizes, one is kidnapping words of another, so to speak. The term comes from Latin *plagium* (kidnapping).

3. What is the only letter of the English alphabet with a name longer than a single syllable?

ENTHUSIASM

Today, if someone is called enthusiastic, it's seen as a compliment. But it wasn't always like that. In the 1840s, Ralph Waldo Emerson wrote, "Everywhere the history of religion betrays a tendency to enthusiasm." At that time, enthusiasm meant being possessed by God or a vain confidence of being divinely inspired. It's from Greek *theos* (god).

CURFEW

In medieval Europe, the *curfew* was a regulation requiring householders to cover or extinguish their fires at a certain hour in the evening, indicated by the ringing of a bell. Why cover the fire? They didn't want people leaving fires burning while everyone was in bed. A conflagration was a bad thing—there were no smoke alarms, no water sprinklers, no fire extinguishers, and no phone to call the fire brigade. Not that there were any fire brigades, either. Curfew was the idea behind preventing infernos like the Great Fire of London. It's from Old French *couvrir* (to cover) + *feu* (fire).

PAVILION

Unlike dandelion, there's no lion in the origin of this word (*dandelion* = *dent de lion*, alluding to the toothed leaves of the plant). There is, however, another creature—a butterfly. That's because the giant roof of a pavilion might look like the wings of a butterfly, and in Latin the word for a butterfly is *papilion*.

4. Here are the names of a few capital cities: pairs, solo, louse, animal, hasten, mail. These are, of course, anagrams of the names. The first one is the capital of France. What are the other corresponding countries?

There's a breed of dogs called papillon because they have ears that look like the wings of a butterfly.

NAUSEA

If you've ever felt sick by the swaying motion of a boat, you've unknowingly experienced the origin of nausea. It came to English from the Greek word *naus*, meaning a "ship." The motion of a ship causes many people to feel sick in the stomach. That's why it's also called motion sickness or seasickness. Other words that have the same origin are *nautical, astronaut, nautilus.*

MUSCLE

Pump iron, grow mice! Well, not real mice, but the word *muscle* does come from the word *mouse.* That's because someone thought that a muscle looked like a little mouse under the skin. In Latin *mus* is a "mouse" and a "little mouse" would be a *musculus.*

COMPANION

A *companion* was someone with whom you broke bread. Once we break this word, we see it's made up of Latin *com-* (together)+*panis* (bread). It's the same *panis* that gave us *pantry.* And a company is, literally speaking, a group of companions.

Chapter 2

Didn't You Just
Make This Up?

When we delay a meeting, we "postpone" it. But if we move a meeting forward, what would we call it? How does "prepone" sound? The word makes perfect sense and it fills a need. It's listed in many dictionaries, including the *Oxford English Dictionary*, but for some reason it has not caught on outside India, where it happens to be an everyday word.

Necessity is the mother of invention, they say, and that's how new words get added to the lexicon. All words are coined words. Someone used them for the first time, in writing or in speech, and thus gave birth to them. Some weather the test of time and get anointed into the venerated pages of dictionaries, while others fade like last year's fashions.

The language mint is always in production. As we speak and write, discuss and debate and chatter and gossip, we generate new words. Sometimes these coinages are helpful additions to the language. At other times, they suffer from excess. There are few words today that haven't had the prefix *cyber-* tacked on to them. Who cares about cybercoffins? (Apparently someone does—the domain name cybercoffin.com is taken.) Same story with the prefix *e-*, though there can be clever coinages—for example, emale: what a woman might call her boyfriend in an online relationship.

A few of the newly minted words stick, others lapse as the language keeps marching on. Here are a few words—coined by known authors—that stuck.

GROK

To understand something thoroughly and intuitively.

All fiction writers invent stories, but some go so far as to invent words to help tell their stories. In his 1961 science fiction novel *Stranger in a Strange Land*, Robert Heinlein told the story of Valentine Michael Smith, an earthling raised by Martians on the Red Planet. Smith returns to Earth and in the process helped us understand what it means to be human.

In the novel, the word is described to have the literal meaning "to drink" in the Martian language. Here is how a character in the novel defines the word: "'Grok' means to understand so thoroughly that the observer becomes a part of the observed-to."

In other words, if you truly understand something, you become one with it. *Grok* can be thought as roughly equivalent to the slang "to dig" in the Martian tongue.

TOXOPHILITE

One who is fond of or expert at archery.

Coined by writer Roger Ascham (1515–1568) as a proper name and the title of his book *Toxophilus*, from Greek *toxon* (bow) + *-philos* (loving). Roger Ascham was the tutor for teenager Elizabeth, later Queen Elizabeth I. His book *Toxophilus* was the first book on archery in English. It was a treatise on archery, but it was also an argument for writing in the vernacular—in English. You could say he shot two birds with one arrow.

The word *toxic* has the same root—it's short for the Greek *toxikon pharmakon*, literally, "bow poison."

ZEITGEBER

An environmental cue, such as light, that helps to regulate an organism's biological clock. It was coined in 1954 by the German physiologist Jürgen Aschoff (1913–1998), from German *Zeit* (time) and *Geber* (giver).

Zeitgebers are events that keep our circadian rhythms regulated. The alternation of the light-dark cycle of a twenty-four-hour day is the most important natural zeitgeber. Another is the earth's magnetic field. An alarm clock is an example of an artificial zeitgeber.

Interestingly, it is claimed that humans' circadian clock has a twenty-five-hour cycle, unlike the earth's twenty-four-hour rotation cycle. In an experiment, subjects lived in a house without windows. There were no external cues, such as a clock, a television, a radio, etc., to give them a hint of when to wake up, or eat, or sleep, and so on. Participants in this study showed a natural rhythm of a twenty-five-hour cycle of sleep, waking up, activity, etc.

Shift work and jet lag owing to rapid travel are some of the activities that can disrupt our circadian rhythms.

SCOFFLAW

One who flouts the law.

Words created for contests rarely survive long, but *scofflaw* is an exception. Language grows by organic change. Thousands of words are coined every year, and only a handful prove their staying power. Marketeers hope the names of their products will become household words. Expensive ads of the Internet company Yahoo! failed to make Yahoo a verb (*"Do you*

5. First and last letters of the name of each of the continents are the same. True or false?

Yahoo!?"). On the other hand, the popularity of the Google search engine made "google" an everyday word without any promotion on their part. Today one might google something, not necessarily on the Internet. In an office you might hear the boss say to John's colleague, "Where's John? I didn't see him in his cubicle today. Could you google him?"

Despite contests, prizes, and ad campaigns, artificially created and promoted words rarely last long, but there are exceptions. Here's a word that came into being as a result of a contest. In 1923, Delcevare King, a rich prohibitionist in Quincy, Massachusetts, announced a contest to coin a word to describe those who flouted prohibition laws. For the winning entry he offered a $200 prize, a considerable sum at the time. Thousands of contestants from the United States and other countries suggested more than twenty-five thousand potential words. Two participants, Henry Dale and Kate Butler, independently came up with the winning word. On January 15, 1923, *scofflaw* was announced as the winning entry. The word has since widened in meaning, and today it's applied to anyone who violates laws, especially those laws that are not easy to enforce. It's rare a word's birth can be pinpointed to a specific day.

A popular but unfounded story goes that the word *quiz* was coined as a result of a bet. According to this tale, in 1791 a Dublin theater manager named James Daly bet that he could introduce a new word into the language within twenty-four hours. Having made the bet, he hired children and gave them a few pieces of chalk with the instruction to write the word *quiz* on the walls around the city. Soon people were wondering what the word meant. It's a great story but it's not true, since

6. What's common among these three words: interrogatives, reinvestigator, tergiversation *(meaning equivocation or evasion).*

the word was recorded many years before the supposed bet took place. The origin of the word remains obscure.

I'd guess the word was coined for use in the game of Scrabble for a score of 22 and up, but alas, that theory doesn't stand the test of time, either—Scrabble was invented much later, in 1938.

TEETOTAL

Choosing to abstain completely from alcohol.

The word was first noted in 1833 in a speech by Richard Turner, an abstinence advocate, in Preston, England. He exhorted members of his temperance society to be teetotal in saying no to alcohol. Was Turner promoting an escape to golf over the attraction of fine spirits? Did he encourage sipping tea instead of wine?

Nope. Turner was simply emphasizing the completeness of the restraint by repeating the first letter of the word total. Though, no doubt, for those fond of drinking, teetotalism reeks of totalitarianism.

Another word that is formed along the same lines is *teetotum*, a small top or a die having four sides. Its name is derived from repeating *t* of *totum* where *totum* is Latin for "all."

Other words coined in this way are *D-day* (the day marked for the beginning of an attack or some other important event) and *H-hour*.

For another instance of a word coined in relation to the temperance movement, see "Cook's tour" in chapter 4, "People Who Became Words."

BLEND WORDS

You can sandwich two existing words (*web* + *master*) or you can blend them: *lexpert* (*lex* + *expert*), someone who is an expert in words. Blending is one of the best and most often used way to coin new words. *Breakfast* and *lunch* fuse into *brunch*;

motel is *motor* plus *hotel*; a *workaholic* is a joining of *work* and *alcoholic*. In blending, sounds, spellings, and meanings of two or more words combine to produce a new word.

When Enron Corporation came down like a house of cards a few years ago, journalists had a field day. They minted the term *Enronomics* to describe the corporation's brand of economics and accounting: off-the-record dealings, cooking books, and numbers sorcery that led to its rise and crash. Creative accounting has been going on for ages, but it seems that Enron took it the furthest ever known to date. The term showed promise, but it didn't last long, perhaps because its pronunciation isn't so obvious.

Lewis Carroll coined many blend words. He even coined a new term to describe those kinds of words. In his *Through the Looking Glass*, Humpty Dumpty explains *slithy* as, "Well, 'slithy' means 'lithe and slimy.' . . . You see it's like a portmanteau—there are two meanings packed up into one word."

Portmanteau is a carrying case for clothes, derived from French *porte* (carries) and *manteau* (cloak). Since then, blend words have also been called portmanteau words.

"Jabberwocky" is a poem in Carroll's *Through the Looking Glass*. It's full of made-up words and contains the line "He chortled in his joy." Interestingly, "Jabberwocky" has been translated into many languages. Not bad for a nonsense poem! The title word *jabberwocky* itself is a coined word, which has come to mean nonsensical language or meaningless speech or writing.

The *Oxford English Dictionary* lists more than a dozen words that were coined by Carroll. Besides *slithy*, here are a few other portmanteaus from Carroll that are now a part of the English language:

Chortle   to laugh in a gleeful manner (a blend of *chuckle* and *snort*)

Frumious   a blend of fuming and furious
Galumph   to move along clumsily (a blend of *gallop* and *triumph*)

GERRYMANDER

To repartition an area to create electoral districts that give an unfair advantage to a political party.

A blend of *Elbridge Gerry* and *salamander*. Massachusetts governor Gerry's party rearranged the electoral district boundaries, and someone thought the newly redistricted Essex County resembled a salamander. Gerry later served as a vice president of the United States (1813–1814).

7. How many words are there in the English language?

~ *Chapter 3* ~

Tasty Words

Many food words are hiding in our daily life: One might have a crummy job, a movie might have a juicy plot, a deal might go sour, and so on. Food is such an essential part of us that we often use food-related terms as metaphors.

Writing is even somewhat like preparing food: careful selection of the ingredients (words), adding them in a deliberate order, assaying the concoction, refining it, and finally serving it. Taste this selection of a few words connected with food.

MADELEINE

1. A small, rich cake baked in a fluted, shell-shaped pan.
2. Something that evokes memory or nostalgia.

If Helen was the woman who launched a thousand ships, a *madeleine* was the cookie that launched a thousand pages, or more. In 1909, as the French writer Marcel Proust dipped his madeleine in tea and tasted it, he was flooded with memories of his childhood. This nostalgia prompted the seven-volume autobiographical novel À *la recherche du temps perdu* (1913–1927), translated as *Remembrance of Things Past* (also as *In Search of Lost Time*). He wrote:

She [Proust's mother] sent for one of those squat, plump little cakes called "petites madeleines," which look as though they had been moulded in the fluted valve of a scallop shell. And soon, mechanically, dispirited after a dreary day with the prospect of a depressing morrow, I raised to my lips a spoonful of the tea in which I had soaked a morsel of the cake. No sooner had the warm liquid mixed with the crumbs touched my palate than a shudder ran through me and I stopped, intent upon the extraordinary thing that was happening to me. . . .

And suddenly the memory revealed itself. The taste was that of the little piece of madeleine which on Sunday mornings at Combray . . . when I went to say good morning to her in her bedroom, my aunt Léonie used to give me, dipping it first in her own cup of tea or tisane.

The name madeleine for this small shell-shaped cookie is a contraction of the French *gâteau à la Madeleine*, literally "Madeleine cake." Who this Madeleine was isn't clear. The recipe for this cake has been attributed to the French cook Madeleine Paulnier/Paumier, but that's unsubstantiated.

The name *Madeleine* itself is derived from *Mary Magdalene*. This Biblical character's name also turned into the word *maudlin*, meaning tearfully sentimental, because she was often depicted as a weeping penitent in paintings.

BAKER'S DOZEN

A group of thirteen.

The term is named because in earlier times in England, bakers often added an extra piece when selling a dozen of anything to safeguard against being penalized for light weight.

8. What do bras have in common with bibles and needles?

MACEDOINE

1. A mixture of diced fruits or vegetables, often served as a salad, appetizer, or dessert.   2. A medley or mixture.

The term is from French *macédoine*, from *Macédoine* (Macedonia), apparently an allusion to the diversity of people in the region that Alexander the Great brought together in his Macedonian empire.

JULIENNE

1. A consommé (clear soup) garnished with thin strips of vegetables.   2. To cut into thin strips.

To *julienne* is to shred a vegetable into small thin strips, the size of an average matchstick. The term is of French origin, derived from the generic use of the first name *Jules* or *Julien* (but not *Julie Anne*). Whether this term was coined after the name of a famous chef is now lost in the mist of time.

Another French term that's coined after someone's name is *bain-marie* (literally, "bath of Mary"), a double boiler. It's a pan with hot water in which a smaller pan is placed for slow cooking. It's derived via French from Medieval Latin *balneum Mariae*, "bath of Maria." Maria was probably an alchemist who devised this technique.

BALSAMIC

1. Fragrant.   2. Soothing or healing.   3. Relating to balsam.

Balsam is any of several aromatic plant resins. Balsamic vinegar, named for its supposed health-giving properties, is a dark, sweet-and-sour vinegar traditionally made in the Modena region in Italy. It's made from white grapes and matured in wooden casks over several years. The term is from Greek *balsamon* (balsam).

Words to Describe People Who Eat

A carefully selected word can have the same effect on a message as the correct seasoning has on a culinary preparation. It can give flavor to the communication or make it unpalatable. There are many words to describe people who enjoy food, and they have fine shades of meaning. It's hard to put them in any particular order, but if one has to, one way would be to arrange them in decreasing order of discrimination, the top one having highly refined tastes and the bottom one being mainly interested in filling the belly:

> *Epicure*
> *Gourmet*
> *Gourmand*
> *Trencherman*

EPICURE

One with refined tastes, especially in matters of food and wine.

An *epicure* is a person who has sophisticated tastes when it comes to food and wine. People considered epicures seem to follow the philosophy of Greek philosopher Epicurus (341–270 BCE). But that's a very narrow definition of the epicurean philosophy. Epicurus identified pleasure as the ultimate goal; he was referring to pleasures of the mind, not pleasures of the body.

Today an epicure might be thought to be the opposite of a stoic, but at one time they were not that far apart in their goals. The big idea was to reduce wants and be free from passion.

GOURMET

A connoisseur of well-prepared food.

A *gourmet* appreciates fine food and wine and is knowledgeable about them. The word is derived from Old French *gromet*, meaning "valet," especially the valet of a wine merchant. A vintner's assistant would be expected to be well informed about wine lore. Later, with influence from *gourmand*, the word took a turn in meaning to its current sense.

Indiscriminate use of the term in advertising has made the term almost meaningless. A restaurant advertising itself as a place for "fine gourmet dining" is almost certain not to be.

GOURMAND

1. One who is fond of good eating.   2. One who enjoys eating to excess.

On the next lower rung of the gastronomic ladder is the *gourmand*. A gourmand could be defined as a gourmet who gets carried away while enjoying all that fine food. *Gourmand* is from Old French *gormant* (glutton).

TRENCHERMAN

A hearty eater.

A *trencherman* is not one who eats like a trencher, nor one who eats trenches full of food. A trencherman is a hearty eater (though all that eating can't be good for the heart). The term derives from *trencher*, a flat piece of wood on which food is served or carved. *Trencher* is from Latin *truncare* (to lop).

* * *

A few more words about food and people:

DEIPNOSOPHIST

A good conversationalist at meals.

---

9. Only one number has all its letters in alphabetical order. And only one number has all its letters in reverse alphabetical order. What are they?

The Greco-Egyptian philosopher Athenaeus wrote the fifteen-volume work *The Deipnosophists* back in the second century. It recounts the dinner-table conversations of learned men who gathered for long discussions. Their talk revolves around food and other topics. Ten volumes of this work survive. They are invaluable in understanding life at the time and from the previous era also because those conversationalists quoted hundreds of other writers.

The word is derived from Greek *deipnon* (meal) and *sophist* (wise or clever man).

ARISTOLOGY

The art or science of dining.

The word has nothing to do with aristocracy (which is from Greek *aristos*, meaning "best"). Nor does it derive from the name of the philosopher Aristotle. Rather, it's from Greek *ariston* (breakfast or lunch) and *logy* (science or study). In author Rex Stout's mystery novels, the obese protagonist detective Nero Wolfe attends the annual dinner of a club named Ten for Aristology. The club's name is explained in the book as "a group of ten men pursuing the ideal of perfection in food and drink."

POSTPRANDIAL

After a meal, especially after dinner.

Postprandial is often used in medicine. In diabetes, one might check the postprandial level of glucose. But the term could be used in almost any context. A postprandial walk is always a good idea. Toastmasters often present postprandial speeches. And a postprandial nap never hurt anyone. The term is from

10. Can you make a word with a letter repeated three times in a row? Hint: try adding -less to a word.

Latin *post-* (after) and *prandium* (meal). Ultimately it's from the Indo-European root *ed-* (to eat or to bite) that has given us other words, such as *edible*, *comestible*, *obese*, *etch*, and *fret*.

The flip side of *postprandial* is *preprandial* (before a meal), and there is *prandial* (relating to a meal) as well.

AVOCADO

The word originated in the Aztec language Nahuatl, where it was called *ahuacatl*, meaning "testicle" because of its shape. When Spanish conquerors invaded South America, they pronounced the name of the fruit as *aguacate*. The name also morphed into *avocado*, influenced by the now obsolete Spanish *avocado*, meaning "lawyer" or "advocate."

Other food-related words that came to English from Nahuatl are *chili* (from *chilli*), *tomato* (from *tomatl*), *cacao* (from *cacahuatl*), *chocolate* (from *xocolatl*, *xococ*: bitter + *atl*: water), *mescal* (from *mexcalli*), and *tamale* (from *tamalli*).

WHEAT

If the word *wheat* sounds similar to the word *white*, it's no coincidence. Both are ultimately derived from Indo-European *kweit-* (white). Wheat is called wheat because it yields white flour when ground.

FRANKENFOOD

Food having genetically modified ingredients.

In 1992, in a letter to the *New York Times* condemning genetic manipulation, English professor Paul Lewis wrote:

> Ever since Mary Shelley's baron rolled his improved human out of the lab, scientists have been bringing just such good things to life. If they want to sell us Frankenfood, perhaps it's time to gather the villagers, light some torches and head to the castle.

Lewis's use of the term *Frankenfood* alluded to the Frankenstein's monster in Mary Shelley's 1818 novel. *Franken-* is a spurious prefix in the sense that the original monster was unnamed. It was the monster's creator who was named Frankenstein; however, popular usage has firmly established the prefix.

What's Hidden in Your Food?

When you wolf down that sandwich, do you know what is hidden in it? As a vegan, I read all food labels and am often surprised to find that a preparation that could easily have been vegan has many animal ingredients in it. I have a rule of thumb: The fewer the ingredients, the more likely it is to be vegan.

As one who writes about words, I have another interest in food words: what's hiding in their etymologies. The words *onion* and *union* differ in only one letter, and there's a reason they are so similar. The word *onion* is derived from *union*, and you can see why if you think about how those numerous scales are united in an onion bulb.

Unlike *onion* and *union*, sometimes the literal meaning of a food name isn't so obvious, especially for names from other languages. *Burrito*, for example, is literally a "little donkey," from Spanish *burro* (donkey) + *ito* (the diminutive affix). Let's look at more words with unusual origins. Sometimes they are named after a shape, at other times for their colors, and often whimsically for something else. Read on to see the literal meanings of these food-related words.

Baguette   stick, from French.
Basmati   fragrant, from Hindi.
Basil   royal, from Greek *basilikos*.
Bonbon   good good, from French *bon*.
Cabbage   head, via French from Latin *caput* (head).

Calzone trouser leg, from Italian.

Candy piece, from Sanskrit *khand* (piece).

Cannoli tube, from Italian, plural of *cannolo*.

Cappuccino Capuchin monk, from Italian. The color of a
 cappuccino resembles that of a friar's habit.

Chimichanga trinket, from Spanish.

Chop suey mixed bits, from Chinese.

Couscous pounded, from Arabic *kaskasa* (to pound).

Croissant crescent, from French.

Daikon large root, from Japanese *dai* (big) and *kon* (root).

Date finger, from Greek *daktulos* (finger), from its shape.

Dim sum dot heart, from Cantonese.

Dolma filling, from Turkish.

Enchilada seasoned with chili, from Spanish *enchilar* (to
 season with chili).

Falafel or *felafel* peppers, from Arabic *falafil*, plural
 of *filfil*.

Gluten glue, from Latin.

Gnocchi a knot in wood, from Italian *nocchio*.

Halibut holy flatfish, from Middle English *hali* (holy) and
 butte (flatfish), because it was eaten on holy days.

Marinara in sailor's style, from Italian.

Meat food. Earlier meat was any food, not necessarily
 animal flesh. That's why sweetmeat is a sweet delicacy,
 not made of animals (but sweetbread is).

Pomegranate seedy apple, from Latin *pomum* (apple)
 granatum (seedy).

Pretzel bracelet, from Latin *bracellus*.

Ragout taste reviver, from French *ragoûter* (to revive the
 taste).

11. What does a checkbook have in common with a cookbook?

Restaurant   feeder or restorer, from French *restaurer* (to feed or to restore). In contrast, the Italian word *trattoria* for a small restaurant that treats, etymologically speaking, from Italian *trattare* (to treat).

Shiitake   oak mushroom, from Japanese *shii* (oak) and *take* (mushroom).

Taco   plug or wad, from Spanish.

Tamarind   Indian date, from Arabic *tamr* (date) and *hindi* (Indian).

Tapas   covers, lids, from Spanish *tapa* (cover or lid). Because in many parts of Spain these snacks are offered with a drink in bars and cafés, often the plate (or the snack itself) is put on top of the drink.

Teriyaki   glaze broil, from Japanese *teri* (glaze) and *yaki* (to broil).

Tofu   fermented beans, from Chinese *dou* (bean) and *fu* (fermented).

Tutti-frutti   all fruit, from Italian *tutta* (all) and *frutta* (fruit).

Vermicelli   little worms, plural of Italian *vermicello*, diminutive of *verme* (worm).

Walnut   foreign nut, from Old English *wealhhnutu*, from *wealh* (Welsh, foreigner) and *hnutu* (nut). It was formerly also known as walsh-nut.

Where Did It Come From?

Often food is named after the place it comes from. *Hamburger* was named after Hamburg, Germany; *Tabasco* sauce after the

---

12. What's the longest word that doesn't repeat a letter? Hint: You can't copyright it.

state of Tabasco in Mexico; *Champagne* wine after the Champagne region in France; and lima beans from the capital of Peru. Here are some words where the place of origin isn't so obvious.

Cantaloupe   after Cantalupo, the name of a former papal villa near Rome, Italy, where the melons were first grown in Europe.

Black forest   after Schwarzwald, a mountainous wooded region in southwest Germany, from German *schwarz* (black) and *Wald* (forest). The region is famous for its clock and toy industries.

Cheddar   after Cheddar, a village in Somerset, England, where this cheese was first made.

Currant   after Corinth, the port in Greece where they originated. Perhaps Corinth had dangerous currents, too.

Habanero   after Havana, Cuba. It's from Spanish *chile habanero* (chili from Havana). Habanero chilies are the hottest of all. (The hotness of chili peppers is measured by the Scoville unit, invented by a chemist named Wilbur Scoville.)

Jalapeño   after Xalapa, the capital of Veracruz State in Mexico. From *chile Jalapeño* (chilies of Xalapa/Jalapa).

Who Gave Them Their Names?

Granny Smith apples came from the name of an Australian woman Maria Ann Smith who developed this variety of apples near Sydney. Many other people are named in food items. Here are a few:

Caesar salad   after Caesar Cardini (1896–1956), a restaurateur in Tijuana, Mexico, who ran a restaurant

named Caesar's. The salad is not named after Julius
Caesar, unless the Roman general was the inspiration
for Cardini's given name.

Graham crackers   after Sylvester Graham (1794–1851),
dietary reformer.

Macadamia nuts   after Australian chemist John Macadam
(1827–1865).

13. What word has st in the middle, in the beginning, and the ending?

~ *Chapter 4* ~

people Who Became Words

Self-improvement author Dale Carnegie once said, "A person's name is to that person the sweetest and most important sound in any language." No wonder we put it to use any chance we get: from naming a business (Wal-Mart) to naming a child (Ron Jr.). For the same reason, some benefactors insist that a hospital auditorium or a park bench carry their names in return for their money.

We name inventions, diseases, countries, products, plants, mountains, planets, and more after people's names. We even coin words after them. Such words are called eponyms, from *epi-* (upon) + *-onym* (name).

The word *eponym* is also used for people who have a word coined after them; for example, Amerigo Vespucci, the Italian explorer after whom America was named. The elementary particle boson is named after Indian physicist Satyendra Nath Bose.

Eponyms are coined after good guys and not-so-good ones. There are thousands of eponyms—plant names, medical terms, city names, country names, and more. Everyday words such as *boycott*, *cereal*, and *ritzy* are eponyms. Here is a glimpse into the world of eponyms.

POTEMKIN VILLAGE

A showy facade designed to mask embarrassing reality.

Imagine a Hollywood set and you'd have a good idea of the original Potemkin village. In 1787, when Catherine the Great, Empress of Russia, visited Ukraine and Crimea, her lover, Prince Grigori Aleksandrovich Potemkin, had some ideas. Grigori, a Russian army officer and statesman, decided to put up elaborate cardboard houses presenting a picture of splendor in the villages.

While this setup presented an illusion of prosperity, the real condition of the village was hidden behind the facade. A *Potemkin village* is, in other words, the idea of whitewash taken to an extreme degree.

While Potemkin is the subject of many a legend, *Potemkin village* is his claim to fame. It refers to an impressive showy facade designed to mask undesirable facts.

CLERIHEW

A humorous, pseudobiographical verse of four lines of uneven length, with the rhyming scheme A-A-B-B, and the first line containing the name of the subject.

Edmund Clerihew Bentley (1875–1956) was a barrister, a reporter, and a writer of detective fiction, but he is known for none of those. Rather, he's famous as the person who originated the *clerihew*, a microbiography in verse.

Here's one of the first clerihews he wrote, apparently while getting bored in a chemistry class:

Sir Humphrey Davy
Abominated gravy.
He lived in the odium
Of having discovered sodium.

Many people have had words coined after their last or first names, but Clerihew is the only one who had a word coined after his middle name. A few more of Clerihew's clerihews:

Sir Christopher Wren
Said, "I am going to dine with some men.
If anyone calls
Say I am designing St. Paul's."

George the Third
Ought never to have occurred.
One can only wonder
At so grotesque a blunder.

MIRANDIZE

To *mirandize* is to advise people under arrest of their legal rights, such as the right to remain silent under questioning, the right to legal counsel, etc. As an adjective, suspects could be read their Miranda rights or given a Miranda warning.

Ernesto A. Miranda (1941–1976) had a record of armed robbery, burglary, and other assorted infractions. After he was arrested for a bank robbery, he signed a written confession.

His conviction was thrown out by the U.S. Supreme Court in 1966, in the case *Miranda v. Arizona*, determining that he had confessed without having been told of his right to remain silent under questioning. The landmark ruling upheld the right against self-incrimination as guaranteed in the Fifth Amendment to the U.S. Constitution.

Miranda's story has an ironic ending: He was later stabbed to death. Police arrested a suspect who chose to remain silent after having been read his Miranda rights. No one was ever convicted.

14. Can you think of what's interesting about the words *rode*, *are, and* came?

ANNIE OAKLEY

A complimentary ticket or a pass to an event.

Phoebe Ann Moses (1860–1926), better known as Annie Oakley, was renowned for her shooting skills. The term was coined from the association of a punched ticket with one of her bullet-riddled targets.

Oakley showed sharpshooting skills at an early age and earned the moniker "Little Sure Shot." Later this shooting star and her husband appeared in the touring "Wild West Show," delighting audiences the world over. Annie was known for amazing feats, such as shooting a coin tossed in the air and knocking the ashes off a cigarette held between her husband's lips. That's perhaps not a bad way to discourage a man from smoking.

In another stunt, she would shoot at a playing card thrown into the air, and before it touched the ground, riddle it with holes (one wonders if chads came out). Someone figured this matched the punched free ticket to an event, and soon all passes became known as *Annie Oakleys*.

MAGINOT LINE

An ineffective line of defense that is relied upon with undue confidence.

This term was coined after André Maginot (1877–1932), French minister of war, who proposed a line of defense along France's border with Germany. Believed to be impregnable, the barrier proved to be irrelevant when Germans went around it and attacked through Belgium in 1940.

15. This capital city's name has three dotted letters in a row (as in the word hijinks). What is this city? No peeking!

FURPHY

A rumor, scuttlebutt.

In the State of Victoria, Australia, the Furphy family makes Furphy carts, for hauling water, trash, etc. These carts were used during World War I, and soldiers used to gather around them and exchange gossip.

This word was formed in much the same way as *scuttlebutt*, a word derived from nautical terminology. A *scuttlebutt* was an open cask of drinking water, around which the crew would swap stories.

PONZI SCHEME

A kind of pyramid scheme: a swindle where money from new investors is given to old ones as the return on their money, to incite them to invest even bigger sums.

If something sounds too good to be true, it probably is. During 1919–1920, Charles Ponzi (1882?–1949), a speculator, offered to double his investors' money in a very short time. Behind his promise of grandiose returns there was no engine of industry to harness human potential and generate revenue.

It was all a facade, using the money of new investors to pay off the previous ones. He claimed to generate revenues by taking advantage of the differences in various currencies used to buy the international reply coupons (IRC), but a later investigation found he had bought only about $30 worth of IRCs.

Soon the bubble burst, and Ponzi's name was forever etched in contemporary parlance as an eponym for such swindles in the investment world where high profits are promised from fictitious sources and early investors are paid off with funds raised from later ones.

COOK'S TOUR

A guided but cursory tour, covering only the main features.

After Thomas Cook (1808–1892), English travel agent. From

cabinetmaking to tourmaking—the story of Thomas Cook is a fascinating account of how this man came to be a trailblazing travel agent. Before he stumbled upon organized travel, Cook worked as a wood-turner, printer, and missionary. He was a champion of the temperance movement, and that led to his career in travel.

In 1841 an important conference of temperance supporters was to be held in Loughborough, UK. Cook convinced the railway company to run a special train for people wishing to attend. Later he conducted excursions to the Paris Exposition of 1855. Eventually he expanded into running tours of Europe, Africa, and beyond, and soon his name become synonymous with travel and tourism.

He may not have made many teetotalers, but he did make many travelers. From selling tickets for a train journey between Leicester and Loughborough for one shilling to a global empire of airplanes, hotels, and tour agencies—now that's a tour de force.

ORWELLIAN

Of or relating to a totalitarian state.

The term evokes George Orwell's novel *1984*, which portrays a futuristic totalitarian state. This word would have been Blairian had English author George Orwell (1903–1950) chosen to write as Eric Arthur Blair, his given name, instead of using a pen name. No matter, it would still be an eponym.

Although Orwell is best known for his satires *Animal Farm* and *1984*, he wrote many compelling essays and articles. In one of his essays, "Politics and the English Language," he translates this verse from Ecclesiastes to show how language can be, and often is, used not only to illuminate but also to obscure:

I returned and saw under the sun, that the race is not to
the swift,

nor the battle to the strong, neither yet bread to the wise, nor yet

riches to men of understanding, nor yet favor to men of skill; but

time and chance happeneth to them all.

And here is how it might appear in bureaucratic English:

Objective consideration of contemporary phenomena compels the conclusion that success or failure in competitive activities exhibits no tendency to be commensurate with innate capacity, but that a considerable element of the unpredictable must invariably be taken into account.

Now how would you want that memo, report, proposal, thesis, letter, or e-mail of yours to read?

MAXWELLIAN

The word has two senses, both good and bad. In the scientific world, *maxwellian* refers to the Scottish physicist James Clerk Maxwell (1831–1879) or his equations and theory in electromagnetism and other fields.

The bad sense of the word—relating to shady business practices, financial tricks, misuse of public funds, etc.—comes from the name of publisher Ian Robert Maxwell (1923–1991).

In the United States we had Ken Lay and friends from Enron; across the pond in the UK, there was Ian Robert Maxwell. Maxwell was a Czechoslovakian-born British publisher who became notorious for misusing his employees' pension funds of some £400 million. He also engaged in dubious transactions

16. *What six-letter word is made up of only two unique letters?*

between his private companies and a public company to prop them up and boost the share prices. For his resilience to rebound after a castigating government report, he earned the nickname "The Bouncing Czech."

GRESHAM'S LAW

The theory that bad money drives good money out of circulation.

Gresham's law says that when both are required to be accepted as legal tender, inferior money remains in circulation while the good money tends to be hoarded or exported.

Examples of bad money could be counterfeit notes, coins that have their edges scraped off to siphon precious metal, or two legal tenders where one is intrinsically superior (for example, a gold coin versus a paper note of the same face value). In general, the law applies to situations outside the financial world as well: for example, bad politicians drive out good ones.

It was coined by economist Henry Dunning Macleod in 1858 after Sir Thomas Gresham (1519–1579), financier and founder of the Royal Exchange in London. Gresham, a financial adviser to Queen Elizabeth I, wrote to her "good and bad coin cannot circulate together."

BENJAMIN

A one-hundred-dollar bill.

Benjamin is a nickname for the U.S. one-hundred-dollar bill. The name derives from Benjamin Franklin, the U.S. statesman whose portrait adorns the bill.

17. When they met for the first time in the Garden of Eden, Adam introduced himself to Eve in a palindrome: "Madam, I'm Adam." How did Eve reply palindromically?

The U.S. currency notes are printed in the Bureau of Engraving and Printing plants in Washington, D.C., and Fort Worth, Texas. I visited the Washington, D.C., money factory a few years back and have to say the place feels a bit surreal. You can see sheets of currency notes rolling through by the millions, as if they were the daily newspaper to be read and discarded. Workers move the giant stacks of uncut sheets with forklifts. No matter how the economy is going, this is one place that always makes money.

It's perhaps fitting that it is Benjamin Franklin (1706–1790), an inventor and printer, whose picture is printed on the highest denomination currency note in circulation in the United States.

ANACREONTIC
Celebrating love and drinking.

The word is coined after Anacreon, a Greek poet in the sixth century BCE, noted for his songs in praise of love and wine. The U.S. national anthem, "The Star-Spangled Banner," is set to the tune of the English song "To Anacreon in Heaven," which was the "constitutional song" of the Anacreontic Society, a gentlemen's music club in London.

GOLDWYNISM
A humorous statement or phrase resulting from the use of incongruous or contradictory words, situations, idioms, etc.

Here are some examples of Goldwynisms:

- Include me out.
- When I want your opinion I will give it to you.
- I'll give you a definite maybe.
- If I could drop dead right now, I would be the happiest man alive.

- Anybody who goes to a psychiatrist ought to have his head examined.
- I may not always be right, but I am never wrong.
- In two words: im-possible.

Continuing the tradition of such eponyms as malapropism, spoonerism, and Goldwynism, will bushism enter the dictionaries as the latest eponym in this category? Only time will tell.

The term is coined from the name of Polish-born U.S. film producer Samuel Goldwyn (1879–1974), who was known for such remarks. Born Schmuel Gelbfisz, he changed his name to Samuel Goldfish after he went to the UK, and then to Samuel Goldwyn after moving to the United States.

KLIEG LIGHT

1. A carbon-arc lamp for producing light, used in moviemaking. 2. The center of public attention.

Klieg light is a modern synonym of the word *limelight*. In earlier times, white lime was used to produce intense light for illuminating the theater stage. Metaphorically, people—famous and infamous—continue to be in the limelight or klieg light, as popular media trains its spotlight on them.

The term is coined after brothers and inventors, lighting experts John H. Kliegl (1869–1959) and Anton T. Kliegl (1872–1927). The last letter *l* of their name apparently became fused with the word *light* in the term *klieg light*.

XANTHIPPE

An ill-tempered woman.

Behind every successful man, there is a woman, they say, and in the case of Socrates, we could credit his wife, Xanthippe. After all, it was Socrates who said, "By all means marry; if you get a good wife, you'll be happy. If you get a bad one, you'll become a philosopher."

After Xanthippe's legendary nagging and scolding, the word has come to refer to any quarrelsome, shrewish woman. Though one has to sympathize with Mrs. Socrates as well—it can't be easy being married to a philosopher. But it's a chicken-and-egg problem: Who knows which came first, philosophizing or peevish scolding?

But then again, anyone who has been named Yellow Mare would grow up to be bitter. Xanthippe is the feminine form of Xanthippos, from Greek *xanthos* (yellow) and *hippos* (horse). Someone xanthodontous has yellow teeth.

In *The Taming of the Shrew*, Katherine is called "As Socrates' Xanthippe, or a worse." In Shakespeare's entire works, Xanthippe is the only word beginning with the letter *x* (excluding Roman numerals).

Astronomers have named an asteroid "156 Xanthippe" in her honor. There's also one called "5450 Sokrates" after the philosopher. Let's hope those asteroids remain on opposite sides of the solar system.

18. What words begin and end with the letters *und*?

~ *Chapter 5* ~

There Is Even a Word for That

With the largest vocabulary of any language, English has a word to describe almost everything. And when we can't find one, we're happy to borrow from another language (from German, *Schadenfreude*—pleasure at others' misfortune), or just make one up (*petrichor*—the pleasant smell of rain after a dry spell).

Having said that, let's not gloat over how many words we have. English's poverty shows in many places; for example, when it comes to words to describe relations. How useful is it to introduce the woman with you as your sister-in-law when the term could mean any number of things?

Here are a few terms that make one say, "I didn't know there was a word for it!" or "Is it really a word?"

AUTOTOMY

Self-amputation or self-surgery.

Autotomy is nature's gift to some animals to help them escape when under attack or injured. A lizard being chased will shed its tail and slip away. The detached tail continues to wriggle, distracting the predator, while its former owner flees to safety. (The lizard goes home and buys a replacement on eBay. Just kidding! Of course, it can't do that—eBay's policy explicitly prohibits lizards from bidding. They just grow it back.)

Other animals who use autotomy are spiders, crabs, lobsters . . . and maybe even humans.

In 2003 a courageous hiker got his arm trapped under a boulder in a remote Utah canyon. He used his pocketknife to cut the arm off and free himself. If only humans could grow parts back too. . . .

The word *autotomy* does double duty. It has another sense: performing surgery upon oneself. It's not as unusual as it sounds. While we see it mostly in science fiction (think of Terminator doing his own eye surgery), with the skyrocketing cost of health care, perhaps days of autotomy aren't far off. Look for do-it-yourself surgery kits in your neighborhood pharmacy soon.

We acquired this word from the Greeks: from *auto-* (self) and *–tomy* (cutting). The word *anatomy* is related. Its derivation refers to the dissection medical students perform to study the structure of a body.

PETRICHOR

The pleasant smell that accompanies the first rain after a dry spell.

The first pitter-patter of raindrops after a long, dry weather is soothing in itself. When the rain brings with it that delightful fragrance, the result is sublime.

In 1964 two Australian researchers, I. J. Bear and R. G. Thomas, needed a word to describe that heavenly smell. Finding none, they coined their own term by combining Greek *petros* (stone) and *ichor* (the fluid that is supposed to flow in the veins of the gods in Greek mythology). An aptly poetic word.

19. What's the only word in the English language that has three apostrophes?

The smell is said to be a concoction of some fifty chemicals from dry plants that are trapped in the earth. With the rain they are released in the atmosphere. I wonder why no one has tried to bottle it for sale.

RESISTENTIALISM

The theory that inanimate objects demonstrate hostile behavior toward us.

If you ever get a feeling that the photocopy machine can sense when you're tense, short of time, need a document copied before an important meeting, and then it breaks down on purpose, you're not alone. Now you know the word for it. As if to prove the point, my normally robust DSL Internet connection went down for two hours just as I was writing this. I'm not making this up!

The word was coined by humorist Paul Jennings as a blend of the Latin *res* (thing), French *resister* (to resist), and *existentialism* (a kind of philosophy).

TROPISM

The turning or bending (typically by growth instead of movement) of an organism in response to an external stimulus.

If you've ever noticed a plant bending toward the light, you've seen an example of *tropism*. The term is usually applied to plants. The response to a stimulus could be positive or negative: toward or away from the stimulus. Some examples of stimuli are light (phototropism or heliotropism), gravity (geotropism), heat (thermotropism), touch (thigmotropism), and water (hydrotropism).

Darwin and his son Francis demonstrated that the tip of the plant detected light, and if you covered just the tip, the plant would grow straight, not toward the light.

The word *tropism* is related to *trope*, the term for rhetorical devices such as metaphor and irony. The idea is that the words in those rhetorical devices are turned in a special way. The word *tropic* came from the same source.

It's derived from Greek *tropos* (turning).

TRICHOLOGY

The science of hair and its diseases.

Whom would you look for when caught in a hairy situation? I'd sure want an expert in *trichology*: the study and treatment of hair and its disorders.

Now, what should we call one who is an expert in trichology: tricho-*something*? Why pull your hair out for a mere word? Let's just call him a "headmaster." If you do often get an urge to pull your hair out, here's a word for the affliction: *trichotillomania.* It comes from a Greek root meaning "father" or "mother of a teen."

Seriously, the Greeks were really the root cause of all this madness: *tricho-* (hair), *-logy* (science, study), *tillein* (to pull out), and *-mania* (madness).

CHIROGRAPHY

The art of handwriting.

Back in the Jurassic era, when there were no laptops and no text-messaging, people used a little thing called a pen to write on a flat surface known as paper. Chirography is a word from those times. It means "handwriting" or "penmanship," also known as calligraphy.

My daughter says, "Why didn't they just download new fonts to their pens?" Well, we did once have fountain pens.

We can thank the Greeks again for the combining forms *chiro-* (hand) and *-graphy* (writing). The word has many cousins:

Chiromancy   reading palms to divine the future: palmistry.

Chiropractic   adjusting the spine (using hands, presumably).

Chiropody   an odd name for podiatry (treating foot problems).

Chiropter   another name for bats (who had their hands retrofitted as wings at Intelligent Design, Inc.).

ACCISMUS

Feigning lack of interest in something while actually desiring it.

If you've ever uttered something resembling any of these expressions, you've practiced the fine art of *accismus*: "Oh, you shouldn't have" or "Thank you, but I'm not worthy of such an honor."

Accismus is showing no interest in something while secretly wanting it. It's a form of irony where one pretends indifference and refuses something while actually wanting it. In Aesop's fable, the fox pretends he doesn't care for the grapes. Caesar, in Shakespeare's *Julius Caesar*, is reported as not accepting the crown. Another example is when a newly elected speaker to parliament is traditionally dragged protesting to take the chair.

The word is from Greek *akkismos* (coyness or affectation).

CEREOLOGIST

One who specializes in investigating crop circles.

Going by the countless varieties of cereals on the supermarket shelves, you'd think you'd have to be a cereologist to be able to select one. But it's not that. Rather, a *cereologist* is

20. What's the shortest word you can spell that uses all the first six letters of the English alphabet?

someone who studies crop circles—mysterious circular patterns on crop fields.

The word is coined after Ceres, goddess of agriculture in Roman mythology.

VAGITUS

The cry of a newborn.

A newborn child's cry is called *vagitus*. Babies' cries have been heard even before birth. It's rare, but *vagitus uterinus* has been observed on occasions when membranes rupture, allowing air to enter the uterine cavity. From Latin *vagire* (to wail).

PARRHESIA

1. Boldness of speech. 2. The practice of asking forgiveness before speaking in this manner.

From political leaders to business executives, very few like to face the truth. Some claim to want candor but follow the dictum of filmmaker Samuel Goldwyn, who said, "I want everybody to tell me the truth, even if it costs them their jobs."

If you're not entirely sure about your boss, I recommend starting with *parrhesia* (sense 2), before giving in to *parrhesia* (sense 1). Preface your opinion of how pinheaded your supervisor's idea is, with:

With all due respect . . .
If I may be so bold . . .

The word is from Greek, from *pan* (all) and *rhesis* (speech).

21. There are not a lot of six-letter words that begin and end with a vowel and don't have any other vowels. This disease's name does, it begins and ends with an a. What is it?

NYCHTHEMERON

A full period of a day and night: twenty-four hours.

Ever wondered why day and night were divided into twelve hours? The number twelve is not as random as it sounds. There are twelve moons in a year. The number twelve is easy to divide into halves, thirds, and quarters. Also, some cultures counted in base twelve: three joints on each finger (thumb as the counter).

Aren't we glad a nychthemeron isn't divided in metric? Who wants to sleep thirty hours every night?

The word is from Greek, a combination of *nykt-* (night) and *hemera* (day).

VELLEITY

Volition at its faintest.

Finally, a word to describe a few of those things we can't wait to do: filling out tax forms, for example. *Velleity* is volition at its weakest. It's a mere wish or inclination, without any accompanying effort. But who could tell just by looking at the word?

So next time you're late in filing your tax return and the tax department sends a reminder, just send them a polite letter vouching for your velleity. The taxman will think the check is coming soon and you've been completely forthright.

It's derived from Latin *velle* (to wish).

DENDROCHRONOLOGY

Tree ring dating.

Dendrochronology is the science of studying tree rings to date past events: climate, the date of construction of a house, etc. This is the idea: Some trees add an annual ring. Each ring is unique as it depends on the climatic conditions during the year. By comparative study of these annual growth rings, dendrochronologists can go back thousands of years and often pinpoint the year quite precisely.

Time imprints on our faces the traces of life we've lived. Laughs, pouts, frowns—all leave their mark. What would facial dendrochronology say about you?

The word is from Greek *dendro-* (tree) and *chronology* (the science of determining dates of past events).

MOGIGRAPHIA

Writer's cramp.

Tennis players have their elbows, athletes have their feet, so what do writers get? They get their cramps. *Mogigraphia* is a fancy name for writer's cramp. Advanced writers go for a mental block. For the ultimate, we recommend carpal tunnel syndrome.

A synonym of *mogigraphia* is *graphospasm*.

The word owes its origin to Greek *mogis* (with difficulty) and *graph* (writing).

TRIBOLOGY

The study of interacting surfaces in relative motion and associated issues, such as friction, lubrication, and wear.

Usually words are coined on the streets of language, but here is one instance where a word may be considered to have been synthesized in a lab, if there could be such a thing as a word lab. In 1965 a group of lubrication engineers decided they needed a name for what they did and contacted the editors of the *Oxford English Dictionary* for help. Out of that came the word *tribology*, suggested by C. G. Hardie, of Magdalen College.

So even though it looks like the perfect word for it, tribology is not the study of tribes. A related term is *triboelectricity*: electricity generated by friction. It's from Greek *tribein* (to rub).

PEDOLOGY

The study of soil: its formation, usage, classification, etc. Also called soil science.

If at first you thought pedology was the study of children, you're not completely off the mark. Using the Greek prefix *pedo-* (child), this term can refer to the field concerned with the development of little ones. But for everyone's sanity, *pedology* is mostly used when referring to soils, and *pediatrics* for children.

Imagine taking your sick child to a pedologist who turns out to be an expert in soils (although he might be able to help with soiled diapers) or expecting a soil specialist to check your backyard when she shows up with a stethoscope around her neck. The word is from Greek *pedon* (soil).

SYNESTHESIA OR SYNAESTHESIA

Sensation crossover: a sensation felt in one sense organ when stimulus is applied to another; for example, visualization of a color on hearing a sound.

Some people seem to have their neural circuits crossed. Someone might see the color green on hearing the note C sharp. Another might feel the sweet taste on seeing something round. This phenomenon is known as *synesthesia*. Many people ascribe various colors, sounds, or smells to particular letters of the alphabet. A reader wrote that she visualized names in colors: "'Anu' is a light pink and 'Garg' is a pinkish tan."

The term also refers to the literary use of an unrelated sense to describe something; for example, warm sounds or fragrant words. Then there is blues music. Well, maybe this thing isn't that unusual. I see red when I hear my neighbor's terrier bark

2.2. The word to describe people from this Pacific island country is a palindrome. What is it?

in the middle of the night. I smell something fishy when I see those Nigerian e-mails offering millions.

The word is derived from New Latin *syn-* (together) and Greek *aisthesis* (sensation or perception).

ANAGNORISIS

The moment of recognition or discovery (in a play, etc.).

If you've ever been to a movie involving two brothers separated at birth, one of whom ends up as a criminal and the other a police officer, you already know about this word. Anagnorisis is the point near the end of the movie when the brothers face each other, notice similar lockets around each other's necks (that their mother gave them at their birth), and discover that they're twins, drop their guns, and hug each other tightly.

Anagnorisis was originally the critical moment in a Greek tragedy, usually accompanied by a *peripeteia* (reversal), leading to the denouement of a story. An example occurs when Oedipus recognizes that the woman he is married to (Jocasta) is really his mother. Aristotle discussed it at length in his *Poetics*. He talked about many different kinds of such recognitions; for example, those by memory, by reasoning, etc. The worst, according to him, is recognition by signs, such as scars, birthmarks, tokens, etc. (including lockets).

The word originated in Greek *anagnorizein* (to recognize or discover).

HA-HA

A sunk fence.

From French *haha*, reduplicative of *ha!*, exclamation of sur-

23. Who was the famous explorer named Cristóbal Colón?

prise, that one might express when tripped by such an obstacle.

In the eighteenth century someone came up with the clever idea of a fence that let the property owner enjoy an unhindered view of the landscape, giving an illusion of contiguous land while protecting him from trespass. A *ha-ha* is a sunk fence, essentially a ditch between two land boundaries that divides the land without obstructing the landscape. Etymologists claim we got the word *ha-ha* from *ha!*, the sound one might exclaim on getting tripped by that trap, otherwise known as a sunken fence, but one can't help thinking it might have been derived from the laughter of a French aristocrat when an unsuspecting guest tripped while being shown the grounds at his château.

ANABIOSIS

A return to life after death or apparent death.

Many animals and plants can survive periods of extreme drought or cold. They reach a state of suspended animation and can come back to life even after being dormant for years. One such plant is the Rose of Jericho, also known as Anastatica or Resurrection plant. In dry conditions, its stems curl into a ball. When blown by the wind, it spreads its seeds along the way. When moistened, it turns into a green plant again, even after years of dryness. The curled ball is sold as a curiosity.

Cryonics is the process of deep-freezing a body for preservation in the hope of possible future revival.

The word is derived from Greek *ana-* (back) and *bio-* (life).

MATERTERAL

Characteristic of, or in the manner of, an aunt.

Materteral is the feminine counterpart of the word *avuncular* (like an uncle). The word has its origin in *maternal aunt*, but now it could be applied to aunts on both sides, just as the word *aunt* originally meant *paternal aunt*, from Latin *amita* (father's sister), from *amare* (to love), but now applies to aunts of both kinds. The word is derived from classical Latin *matertera* (maternal aunt), from *mater* (mother).

If instead of "in the manner of an aunt," you want to describe "in the manner of an ant" the word is formic, from Latin *formica* (ant).

THANK-YOU-MA'AM

A bump or depression in a road.

Here's a colorful word for those potholes and bumps in roads that jar a vehicle's occupants. But why *thank-you-ma'am*? There are various explanations. It could be from the nod of the head that results when one passes over a bump or depression in a vehicle. That nod was taken as if in an acknowledgment of a favor. Another theory suggests that when a man and the object of his affection rode in a coach, any bump brought the man and the woman closer, initiating a brief pleasurable contact, thus the term alludes to the supposed thank-you from the man.

Whatever the origin, there's still scope to bring this charming term back, even though Victorian coaches are long gone and roads are much better. Why not use it to describe the modern traffic-calming device variously called a speed bump or speed-breaker?

In Oliver Wendell Holmes's 1868 novel, *The Guardian Angel*, Mrs. Hopkins says: "We all have our troubles. It isn't everybody that can ride to heaven in a C-spring shay, as my poor husband used to say; and life's a road that's got a good many thank-you-ma'ams to go bumpin' over, says he."

24. Why are English letters called "uppercase" or "lowercase?"

Chapter 6

Fictional Characters Who Came Alive

One of the most important ingredients of fiction is its characters. Think of any memorable book, play, or movie, and you'll recall its people—from protagonist (and deuteragonist and tritagonist and . . .) to antagonist. These are the folks one can feel, relate to, though not necessarily always agree with.

In the hands of a capable writer, these imaginary people have depths—they are not cardboard characters. With all their foibles, follies, and victories, they come alive on the pages of a book and in the mind of the reader. Perhaps the ultimate sign of their character is that they live on in the pages of dictionaries.

Words derived from someone's name are called eponyms, from *epi-* (upon) + *-onym* (name). There are countless real people after whose name eponyms are coined: Charles Boycott of Ireland gave us *boycott*, George Orwell of *1984* fame brought us *Orwellian*, and sharpshooter Annie Oakley gave us another term for a free ticket.

Now we'll discuss fictional persons who came alive and added a bit more color to our language.

DRYASDUST

Extremely dull, dry, or boring.

The word refers to Jonas Dryasdust, a fictitious person to whom Sir Walter Scott (1771–1832) dedicated some of his novels. At the beginning of the novel *Ivanhoe*, Sir Walter wrote:

DEDICATORY EPISTLE
TO
THE REV. DR. DRYASDUST, F.A.S.

Dr. Dryasdust, however, was the writer's own creation. He pretends to dedicate the novel to him for having supplied him with dry historical details. Since then, the term is used to describe a person devoted to dry, uninteresting details. Dryasdust—*dry as dust*—is obviously a charactonym (a name that is descriptive of a character trait).

DRAWCANSIR

A blustering, bragging bully.

This word was born of a literary rivalry. Drawcansir was the name of a character in the play *The Rehearsal* (1671) by George Villiers (1628–1687), second duke of Buckingham. The character was apparently named for his potvaliant (showing courage under the influence of drink) tendencies: draw can (of liquor). The play was a satire on poet John Dryden's inflated tragedies. The character Drawcansir was modeled as a parody of Almanzor in Dryden's *Conquest of Granada*. Dryden in turn lampooned Villiers in a passage in his poem *Absalom and Achitophel* (1681).

ABIGAIL

A lady's maid.

After Abigail, an attendant in *The Scornful Lady* (1610), a play by Francis Beaumont and John Fletcher. She was probably named after the biblical character Abigail the Carmelitess, who often called herself a handmaid. The name *Abigail* derives from Hebrew *Avigayil*, meaning "father's joy."

BONIFACE

An innkeeper.

Boniface was a jovial innkeeper in the 1707 comedy *The Beaux' Stratagem* by the playwright George Farquhar (1678–1707).

LADY BOUNTIFUL

Someone, especially a woman, known for charity and generosity.

Here's another eponym from *Beaux' Stratagem*. Lady Bountiful was a character noted for her kindness and gracious generosity. This is how the character Will Boniface describes Lady Bountiful:

> My lady Bountiful is one of the best of women. Her late husband, Sir Charles Bountiful, left her with £1000 a year; and I believe she lays out one-half on't in charitable uses for the good of her neighbours. In short, she has cured more people in and about Lichfield within ten years than the doctors have killed in twenty; and that's a bold word.

The term is sometimes used in a pejorative way to indicate a woman who is ostentatious about giving. Here's an example from a newspaper article discussing a giveaway on the program

25. Orthographically speaking, what do the two countries Afghanistan and Tuvalu have in common?

of television talk-show host Oprah Winfrey. She had arranged each of the hundreds of audience members in her show that day to receive a free car, thanks to auto manufacturer General Motors: "Of course, Oprah didn't spend a penny to look like Lady Bountiful. The giveaway cost General Motors in the vicinity of US $6 million."*

SIMON-PURE

Genuinely pure; also used to describe an amateur as opposed to a professional.

This term is from the phrase "the real Simon Pure," after a character named Simon Pure who was impersonated by another in the play *A Bold Stroke for a Wife*, by Susannah Centlivre (1669–1723). This term is used sometimes to refer to someone who is pretentiously or hypocritically virtuous.

COLONEL BLIMP

A pompous reactionary with out-of-date views.

We got this term after Colonel Blimp, a cartoon character created by New Zealand–born British cartoonist David Low (1891–1963). Colonel Blimp was an obese, walrus-mustached character whose pompous, jingoistic pronouncements became a symbol of unthinking patriotism.

HEATH ROBINSON

Absurdly complex and fancifully impractical.

The term was coined after W. Heath Robinson (1872–1944), a British artist known for drawing ingeniously complicated devices.

*Anne Kingston, "The Boardroom as Billboard," *National Post* (Canada), October 14, 2004.

It's not only mechanical devices that can be Heath Robinsonish. A few years back I came across a book titled *How to Wash Your Face*. I'm not kidding—this 256-page tome was written by a doctor and retailed for $25. They say truth is stranger than fiction. The fiction that comes to mind here is a Heath Robinson contraption.

Who knows? Those illustrations might make you laugh, resulting in the coffee in your mug getting spilled on the tail of the pet cat on your lap, making the startled kitty jump and hit the ceiling, thus activating the fire-sprinkler and causing it to trigger the fire alarm, making you look up in curiosity, so that your face is splashed with the water from the sprinkler, thus saving you the $25 cost of the aforementioned book. Who said those devices were useless?

Cartoonist Rube Goldberg (1883–1970) was the American counterpart of Heath Robinson.

YELLOW JOURNALISM
Sensational journalism.

A cartoon character lies behind this brand of journalism that employs exaggeration, scandals, and lurid stories to attract readers. The term arose from the Yellow Kid, the lead character in *Hogan's Alley*, a comic strip that debuted in the 1890s and was wildly popular. The artist behind the comic strip moved from the *New York World*, a newspaper owned by Joseph Pulitzer, to William Randolph Hearst's *New York Journal*. Pulitzer hired another artist, and for a while both newspapers were running two versions of the strip.

The Yellow Kid was the object of a circulation war

26. What's the only letter in the alphabet that does not appear in the name of any state in the United States?

between the two newspapers that eventually resulted in both engaging in journalistic practices characterized by hyperbole, melodrama, and even reporting fictitious events as news.

It's ironic that Joseph Pulitzer, owner of a newspaper known for sensationalistic reporting during his lifetime, has provided the eponym behind the most respected journalism award in the United States.

There are other examples of softening of image with the passage of time and the institution of awards. Alfred Nobel, who invented dynamite, is now better known for his Nobel Peace Prize. Maybe one day an annual Gates Prize will be instituted to be given to the company most admired for its fair business practices.

SAD SACK

A well-meaning but hopelessly inept person, especially a soldier.

After the cartoon character created by cartoonist George Baker (1915–1975) during World War II. George Baker was a Disney artist, and thanks to the war draft he found himself in the army. Sgt. George Baker drew the Sad Sack character and it became a regular feature in the U.S. army weekly *Yank*.

Sad Sack is a bungler, a blunderer, a botcher, a bumbler, a classic schlemiel (as the story goes, a schlemiel is one who always spills his soup; schlimazel is the one on whom it always lands).

27. Kangaroo words carry a little joey—a smaller version of themselves within their spellings: respite has rest, matches has mates. What are the joey words in these kangaroo words: curtail, regulates, splotch, deceased.

MITTY

An ordinary, timid person who indulges in daydreams involving great adventures and triumphs.

After the title character in *The Secret Life of Walter Mitty*, a short story by James Thurber, later made into a movie (1947) of the same name. Thurber's story appeared in the March 18, 1939, issue of the *New Yorker*. Walter Mitty is a meek husband, rather uxorious, who fantasizes of great exploits to escape the humdrum of daily life. One minute he is dreaming of being a heroic pilot ("Throw on the power lights! Rev her up to 8500!"), the next minute he becomes a daring naval commander. In his next thought he transforms into a master surgeon, and even a cool killer.

PRUFROCKIAN

Marked by timidity and indecisiveness, and beset by unfulfilled aspirations.

This word is coined after the title character in T. S. Eliot's poem "The Love Song of J. Alfred Prufrock." Prufrock, the aging hero of Eliot's 1915 poem, is haunted by his cautious, hesitant approach to life and his conforming existence: "I have measured out my life with coffee spoons."

He wonders about the possible romances he didn't dare broach, "Do I dare disturb the universe?"

If only he knew Tennyson's lines written in 1850:

'Tis better to have loved and lost
Than never to have loved at all.

SHERLOCK

A detective or a person who is good at solving mysteries.

After Sherlock Holmes, a fictional detective in the works

of Arthur Conan Doyle (1859–1930). Although Sherlock Holmes was a fictional character, his many fans, who often call themselves Baker Street Irregulars, sometimes pretend he was real.

CRINGEWORTHY

Causing extreme embarrassment.

The term was popularized by Cuthbert Cringeworthy, a character in the British comic strip *The Bash Street Kids*. Cuthbert is the brightest kid in the class, a bespectacled, hardworking Brit (I thought that was Harry Potter). Wait, Cuthbert is also bossy and rude. He is a teacher's pet and looks exactly like him. No one wants to be seen with him. Clearly, Cringeworthy is a charactonym, a name that suggests personality traits of a character.

The word *cringe* is from Old English *cringan* (to yield or shrink). So someone cringeworthy makes you feel crinkled, etymologically speaking.

POINDEXTER

An extremely intelligent but socially inept person.

This word is coined after Poindexter, a character in the animated series *Felix the Cat*. Poindexter is a synonym of nerd or geek. In the cartoon, Poindexter is the nephew of The Professor, the archenemy of Felix the Cat. The creator of the cartoon series is said to have named the character Poindexter after his lawyer.

THROTTLEBOTTOM

A purposeless incompetent in public office.

The term refers to Alexander Throttlebottom, a vice presidential character in the musical comedy *Of Thee I Sing*. There's the Presidents' Day to honor presidents, but what about their deputies, the vice presidents? It's about time we paid our dues to the vice president, too. A VP, by very nature, is meant to play second fiddle, and that's not easy. John Adams, who had the (mis)fortune to be the vice president for two terms (under George Washington), described his position as "the most insignificant office that ever the invention of man contrived or his imagination conceived."

Dan Quayle, vice president during the George H. W. Bush administration said, "One word sums up probably the responsibility of any vice president, and that one word is 'to be prepared.'"

Here's how the term *throttlebottom* came to represent VPs and other similar (mostly) harmless figures:

The first musical comedy to win the Pulitzer Prize, *Of Thee I Sing*, is a brilliant political satire that gave us this word. In this masterly operetta (music: George Gershwin; lyrics: Ira Gershwin; libretto: George Kaufman and Morris Ryskind), presidential candidate John P. Wintergreen runs a political campaign based on the theme of love.

His National Party sponsors a beauty contest, with Wintergreen to marry the winner. Instead, Wintergreen falls in love with Mary Turner, a secretary at the pageant, and marries her on the day of his inauguration.

Diana Devereaux, the contest winner, sues President Wintergreen for breach of contract; France threatens to go to war, since Devereaux is of French descent; and Congress impeaches him.

Wintergreen points out the U.S. Constitution's provision that when the president is unable to perform his duty, the vice president fulfills the obligations. VP Throttlebottom agrees to marry Diana and forever etches his name in the dictionaries.

28. What's the only country in Africa that has Spanish as one of its official languages?

ZELIG

A chameleon-like person who can change his or her persona to fit in any surrounding; one who appears to be present everywhere and to be unexpectedly associated with famous people or events.

After Leonard Zelig, hero of the 1983 film *Zelig*, by Woody Allen. In this movie, Zelig can blend in with people around him: If he is with doctors he can transform himself into a doctor. He can take on the characteristics of anyone—a Hassidic rabbi, someone obese, a Scot, and so on. The name Zelig is from German *selig* (blessed, happy).

DARBY AND JOAN

A devoted old couple leading a quiet, uneventful life.

The term is coined after a couple named in an eighteenth-century poem in the *Gentleman's Magazine*. In 1735 Henry Woodfall, a printer's apprentice, wrote a ballad entitled "The Joys of Love Never Forgot," about a happily married elderly couple. His inspiration for these characters was his own boss John Darby and his wife, Joan:

> Old Darby, with Joan by his side,
> You've often regarded with wonder:
> He's dropsical, she is sore-eyed,
> Yet they're never happy asunder . . .

As one can imagine, he wrote the poem after Darby's death. It in turn inspired follow-up poems, and eventually Darby and Joan became a metaphor for a happily married old couple leading a quiet life. In the UK, clubs for old people are still called Darby and Joan clubs.

29. What's the origin of the name Lego (toys)?

~ Chapter 7 ~

You Have Changed!

In his 1704 satire A *Tale of a Tub*, Jonathan Swift wrote, "This I am told by a very skilful computer, who hath given a full demonstration of it from rules of arithmetic." Back then—more than three hundred years ago—there were no computers. There was not even electric power as we know it. Was Swift being prescient?

The London newspaper *Westminster Gazette* wrote in a 1909 piece, "Mr. Lockhart, having 'googled' to no purpose . . ." There was no Google search engine at the time. There was nothing to google—the Web hadn't even been invented yet. What is going on here? Are we in a time warp?

What's going on is a demonstration of the infinite adaptability of a language where one can change the meanings of the words to fit the times. Back in Swift's era, a computer was some "one" (not some "thing") who did the mind-numbing task of adding, subtracting, multiplying, and dividing as his day job. He was a reckoner. He was a calculator (there we go again—a *calculator* was a human, too). With the arrival of computing machines—computers—we outsourced the job of humans to machines and continued using the same word.

In the *Westminster Gazette* story, Mr. Lockhart is a cricket player who sends a googly—a trick delivery of a cricket ball.

The verb *to google* was backformed from the word *googly* (lexicographers are not certain where the word *googly* came from), just as nearly a century later we formed another verb *to google* from the name of the search engine. Unlike what happened to *computer*, here we coined the word *google* unaware that there was an existing word with another meaning.

Time changes all things, including words. While two senses of *google* were formed independently, more often a word travels through time gradually changing its meaning, even taking an entirely opposite meaning. Sometimes a word can get very specific. Sometimes it becomes a generic.

A dictionary is only a snapshot of a language. It's out of date the moment after the picture is taken. Fortunately, language change is slow, like the movement of a glacier. We can't see it happening from day to day, but over the course of decades or centuries it becomes obvious.

Here's a look at some of the words where the change is especially marked. Let's contrast their old sepia pictures with modern color photographs.

SILLY

Imagine you got hold of a time machine and went back some seven hundred years. You walk into the town square and bump into the locals. With your jeans, T-shirt, and iPod you stand out among the villagers of the fourteenth century. Some call you *silly*. Other think you are *nice*. Which ones are complimenting you? Which ones think you're witless?

Well, things are not what they seem. *Silly* started life as *seely*, and it meant "blessed," "pious," "good." Over the centuries, the sense shifted. *Good* and *pious* became *harmless* and *innocent*. Then *harmless* became *defenseless* or *helpless*. And someone *helpless* was probably insignificant and feeble. Maybe unsophisticated, a rustic. Perhaps someone ignorant. From there it didn't take much for the sense of the word to morph into *stupid*. From being *blessed* to being *ridiculous*? Who would have thought?

The word *nice* took an opposite route, sort of. Back then, someone *nice* was a foolish fellow. Chaucer wrote, "If it be ony fool or nyce, In whom that Shame hath no justice." Though along the way, it took senses spanning almost the whole spectrum of human qualities: foolish, simple, dissolute, extravagant, scrupulous, elegant, fastidious, refined, respectable, fainthearted, lazy, fragile, pampered, strange, shy, intricate, exact, slender, trivial, dexterous, attractive, and, finally, pleasant and agreeable. Nice! With so many senses we could describe every one of the 6 billion people on this earth. Who needs another word?

And it all started with the Latin *ne-* (not) + *scire* (to know). Someone nice was ignorant. In Spanish, *necio* still means "foolish" or "fool." That same Latin root gave us *science*, *prescient*, *plebiscite*, *conscious*, and *conscience*.

DEMAGOGUE

Today a demagogue is one who appeals to the prejudices and emotions of the people to gain power. It came from Greek *demagogos* (leader of the people), from *demos* (people) + *agogos* (leader). In ancient Greece, a *demagogos* was a popular leader, and the word was free of any negative connotations. With time, the term became negative. Now no self-respecting politician would like to be called a demagogue, no matter how often he uses words such as *patriotism*, *honor*, *courage*, and *sacrifice* in trying to sway people.

BELDAM

Today *beldam* is an ugly old woman, but in the beginning it was a *grandmother*. Poet Michael Drayton wrote in 1613:

30. Can you think of an instance where an abbreviation has more syllables than its full form?

"The beldam and the girl, the grandsire and the boy." The word is a combination of the French *belle* (fair) and *dame* (lady). Later it began to be applied to any old woman. Eventually it took a wrong turn on the linguistic highway and ended up in the verbal ghetto. A word to describe a loving, wise old woman became a word for an ugly old hag. Today be prepared for a severe thrashing with a broomstick if you dare to call a woman a beldam.

In French, a mother-in-law is still called a *belle-mère*, literally "beautiful mother." No wonder French was once the language of diplomacy. Though we are not entirely sure if French women secretly regard their *belles-mères* in the old sense of *beldam* or the new. Incidentally, in English the term *mother-in-law* is an anagram of *woman Hitler*.

There's a poisonous plant called belladonna (also known as deadly nightshade), from the Italian *bella* (fair) and *donna* (lady). It's so called because women once used the plant extract as a cosmetic. They used to put a few drops in their eyes to dilate the pupils, apparently making them more attractive. Today you'd think they were drunk, or on drugs.

FEISTY

Having seen a few words that have been demoted, let's go to one that has lowly origins but is now a positive word. One who is *feisty* is full of energy, someone who's spunky, someone who's spirited. It all started from *fist*, which in earlier times meant to discharge gaseous matter from the nether regions.

The word began to be used for a small mixed-breed dog, as in *fisty cur* or *fisty hound*. From the snappy look of the dogs, it began

31. What's the longest word you can find that has the same phonetic and regular spelling?

to be applied to humans as well. The word does have negative senses, too: touchy, irritable, though these are not as common.

RESENT

Resent was a neutral word in the beginning. We got it from French *ressentir*, meaning "to feel" (love, sorrow, joy, etc.). In French it's still a neutral word. This 1648 citation from the *OED* shows *resent* in its earlier sense: "God resents an infinite satisfaction in the Accomplishment of his own Will."

EGREGIOUS

As recently as 1855, *egregious* was someone remarkable in a good way, as in this line from William Makepeace Thackeray: "When he wanted to draw . . . some one splendid and egregious, it was Clive he took for a model." Today *egregious* is used only for the most flagrant, most outrageous conduct.

The word literally means "out of the flock," from *ex-* (out of) + *grex* (flock). Earlier someone who stood out for commendable behavior was called egregious, now it's for reprehensible conduct. Perhaps our times reflect this: Earlier heroes and heroines were those who gave themselves up in selfless sacrifices. Today we admire self-worshiping movie actors, convicted rap singers, and greedy CEOs.

The word *notorious* followed a similar route. Once upon a time it was neutral or it could be positive, from Latin *notus* (known). With the passage of time it acquired a darker shade. But even today there are times we use this word with a positive connotation ("He is a notorious punster and people love him").

HARLOT

The word started out as a term to describe a vagabond, a young good-for-nothing fellow. Then it evolved, and a *harlot* could be either a vagabond, a menial servant, a clown or a juggler who made others laugh, a ballet dancer. Slowly the word fell from grace, and it was applied to someone lascivious, male or female. Finally, it became specific only to women. The word is from Old French.

NERVOUS

When it first entered the language, the word had the literal meaning of sinewy and tough, as related to the body. Something or someone *nervous* was strong, tough, and bold. We still use the word *nerve* in that sense, as in, "He had the nerve to say no to the king."

At a later point the word began to be applied metaphorically, as the poet William Cowper said about writing in 1780: "Whatever is short should be nervous, masculine, and compact." Today no one wishing to appear strong would like to be called *nervous*.

LEECH

Who would have thought that *leech* was once a word for a physician? Since leeching was the preferred treatment method of doctors in the past, the word began to apply to those bloodsucking worms as well. Yes, the worm got the name after the healer. Though even now, it's applied in some cases—a veterinarian who treats horses is still called a horse-leech.

With the return of leeches to medical use lately, maybe it's time to restore this word to the medical profession. But then, whether we use this word or not, the exorbitant bills from a doctor do make one feel as if being bled by a leech.

The word *doctor* derives from Latin *docere* (to teach), and earlier a doctor was someone who taught something, not necessarily medicine. In Italian, *Dottore* is a commonly used expression of respect, used to address anyone who graduated from university. The equivalent term for women is *Dottoressa*.

And while we are on the topic, etymologically speaking, a *surgeon* is not much different from a *chiropractor*, no matter how much a surgeon looks down his nose at a chiropractor. Both derive from Greek *chiro-* (hand). So surgeons were people who do healing manually, using their hands. Even with the advances in medical technology, this literal definition of a surgeon stands. In French, a *surgeon* is known as *chirurgien*. In Spanish, it's *cirujano*.

The Greek word for hand—*manus*—gave us a word that has turned around over time: *manufacture*. At one time it meant to make something by hand, as a manuscript is a document written by hand. These days, manufacturing is usually done by a machine.

GARBLE

Today if you *garble* something, you muddle it—you do almost the opposite of what garble meant in the beginning. Originally, *to garble* was to remove refuse from something—from spices, for example. More generally, to garble was to pick the best from something. English speakers of times gone by misused the word, "garbled" the sense of the word, you might say. Eventually the word came to refer to the jumbling of something.

SYCOPHANT

From Greek *phainein* (to show) came the word *sycophant*, and it meant "informer." Then the word took the figurative sense of a slanderer, a reverse of what it means today: a servile flatterer. Old sense or new, it's best to be far away from a sycophant.

NIECE

A *niece* was once a granddaughter, from Latin *neptis*. A *nephew*, on the other hand, was a grandson, from Latin *nepos*. It's the same nepos that brought us *nepotism*.

> *32.* This Russian-born author named a character as Vivian Darkbloom in his most famous novel. This character's name is an anagram of his own name. Who is this author?

* * *

Now that we are visiting relatives, let's stop to look at a few others. Today a *sibling* is a brother or sister, but once it was any relative. Derived from Old English *sib* (kinship), it's the same *sib* that gave us the word *gossip*. *Gossip* is a contraction of *god's sib*. A *gossip* used to be a word for a godfather or godmother.

Naturalist and prolific author Thomas Pennant wrote in his 1778 book, *Tour in Wales*: "The gossips . . . were doubtlessly rich persons." From the way stories flow between relatives and acquaintances near and far, the term picked up the sense of idle chat.

A story circulating on the Internet claims that the origin of the word *gossip* is in the olden days' practice of maids sent to taverns to "go sip" some ale and pick up some juicy stories about the neighbors along the way. That sounds like a fascinating way to learn about the neighborhood talk, back when there was no e-mail or phone: "You go sip there." Talk about an easy maiden life in those olden days! It's a good story but much like a lot of gossip, it's not true.

* * *

The story goes that when St. Paul's Cathedral was finished and the architect Sir Christopher Wren showed it to King James II, the king pronounced the edifice "amusing, awful, and artificial." The architect was delighted, for the king's words meant "amazing, awe-inspiring, and artful" at that time.

Wonder what "amusing, awful, and artificial" will mean five hundred years from now.

33. What's the only state in the United States with a name just one syllable long?

~ Chapter 8 ~

Dickensian Characters Who Became Words

What's the yardstick for a fictional work's success in your book? A hefty advance, rave reviews, or a sale in millions? A feat only very few works can claim is that a character from them has become a word in the dictionary. With that measure in mind, novelist Charles Dickens (1812–1870) would have to head the list. Dozens of his characters have taken on lives of their own and are now immortalized in the pages of English-language dictionaries.

Dickens created nearly a thousand characters in his fictional worlds. Some of them were based on real-life people (which got him in trouble), but all had unforgettable names, such as M'Choakumchild (a schoolmaster in *Hard Times*), Paul Sweedlepipe (a landlord in *Martin Chuzzlewit*), and Luke Honeythunder (a character in his last, unfinished novel, *The Mystery of Edwin Drood*). And who can forget a name like Pecksniff?

Here is a look at a few of those memorable Dickensian characters who made it into the dictionaries.

PICKWICKIAN

Pickwickian refers to someone having the qualities of generosity, kindness, and naïveté. It's from the title character of

Dickens's first novel, *The Pickwick Papers*. Samuel Pickwick, usually called Mr. Pickwick, is the founder of the Pickwick Club. He's short and plump and known for his simplicity and kindness.

The word *pickwickian* has another meaning. It's applied to a word or phrase that's meant not to be taken literally, presumably to avoid giving or taking offense. It's often used in the expression "in a Pickwickian sense."

Mr. Pickwick accuses Mr. Blotton, a member of the Pickwick Club, of behaving in a "vile and calumnious mode." Mr. Blotton returns the favor by calling him "humbug." Later it's made clear that "he entertained the highest regard and esteem for the honourable gentleman; he had merely considered him a humbug in a Pickwickian point of view."

Well, *pickwickian* is a hardworking word—it's doing triple duty. There's a medical condition known as Pickwickian syndrome. It's a combination of obesity, sleepiness, and irregular breathing. The term alludes to Joe "fat boy," a rotund character in *The Pickwick Papers* who is notorious for falling asleep, even while knocking at a door. The National Sleep Foundation has set up a Pickwick Fellowship, which makes grants to study sleep disorders. So this sense isn't coined from Mr. Pickwick; rather, it's from the title of the novel.

WELLERISM

An expression involving a familiar proverb or quotation and its facetious sequel. It's usually composed of three parts: a statement (often a proverb), the speaker, and the situation that gives the statement an ironic twist.

Examples:

"Everyone to his own liking," the old woman said when she kissed her cow.

"We'll have to rehearse that," said the undertaker as the coffin fell out of the car.

"Prevention is better than cure," said the pig when it ran away from the butcher.

"The suspense will kill me," said the man about to be hanged.

The term is named after Mr. Pickwick's servant Samuel Weller and his loquacious father, Tony Weller, known for such utterances in *The Pickwick Papers*. The novel appeared in a serialized form, and when readers' interest began to flag, Dickens introduced the Wellers into the story. They could be credited with reviving readers' interest and saving Dickens's writing career.

A few Wellerisms from *The Pickwick Papers*:

"Out vith it, as the father said to the child, wen he swallowed a farden" (farden = farthing).

"What the devil do you want with me, as the man said, wen he see the ghost."

"Hooroar for the principle, as the money-lender said ven he vouldn't renew the bill."

STIGGINS

A pious impostor.

The Reverend Stiggins is a hypocritical shepherd of a Temperance Association in *The Pickwick Papers*. His red nose betrays his true inclinations. Here's how Dickens describes him: "He was a prim-faced, red-nosed man, with a long, thin countenance,

34. *These two superlative words are opposites, yet their verb forms are synonyms. What are they?*

and a semi-rattlesnake sort of eye—rather sharp, but decidedly bad." "Semi-rattlesnake sort of eye"? With that kind of image, we know Stiggins can't be up to any good.

FAGIN

Someone who trains others, especially children, in crime.

In *Oliver Twist*, Fagin is the leader of a gang of pickpockets. When Oliver runs away from the cruelty of an undertaker to whom he was apprenticed, he ends up in Fagin's gang, where he joins other orphaned children who are taught the art of stealing and picking pockets. The Artful Dodger was among Fagin's protégés.

Dickens modeled Fagin as a Jew, and his character of a sinister, creepy fellow reflects the pervasive anti-Semitism of the time. Famed comic artist Will Eisner felt so strongly about this stereotype that he created a graphic novel, *Fagin the Jew*, in which he told Fagin's story from Fagin's point of view.

Profiling the legendary biblioklept Stephen Blumberg ("the greatest book thief in U.S. history"), the *New Yorker* magazine writes, "He was a fagin. Many of his friendships were with adolescent boys. He gave them money to help him unload his truck and sometimes to steal things."

BUMBLEDOM

Behavior shown by petty officials: fussiness, pomposity, arrogance, inefficiency, etc.

Bumbledom is another term that originated in *Oliver Twist*. It's from Bumble, a minor parish official who manages the workhouse where Oliver was born. From this character, *bumbledom* has come to represent manners and actions of a

35. What's the longest one-syllable word you can think of?

bureaucratic government official or someone in a petty position. It's the same Bumble who gave us the immortal line, "The law is a[n] ass."

The behavior of people who make bumbledom was explained well by the author and historian C. Northcote Parkinson, who said, "The man who is denied the opportunity of taking decisions of importance begins to regard as important the decisions he is allowed to take." It's the same Parkinson of Parkinson's law fame: "Work expands to fill the time alloted for its completion."

URIAH HEEP

A hypocritically humble person.

Uriah Heep is the clerk in Dickens's autobiographical novel, *David Copperfield*. He pretends humility and addresses David as "Master Copperfield," but his insincerity is apparent. He works for the lawyer Mr. Wickfield. He claims to be a humble person ("I am well aware that I am the umblest person going") while in reality he is a scheming character who makes his way to become a partner of Mr. Wickfield. He is exposed by Micawber.

MICAWBER

An impractical optimist.

Wilkins Micawber, a character in *David Copperfield*, is an eternal optimist. He is impoverished but always hopeful "something will turn up." He makes great speeches, though: "Annual income twenty pounds, annual expenditure nineteen nineteen and six, result happiness. Annual income twenty pounds, annual expenditure twenty pounds ought and six, result misery." Dickens modeled Micawber's character after his father, whose inability to pay his debts sent him to prison and little Dickens to a shoe-polish factory.

DOLLY VARDEN

A style of dress; a species of trout.

Dolly Varden is a colorful character in *Barnaby Rudge*. A locksmith's daughter, she is flirtatious and loves to wear beautiful, flashy dresses. The popularity of her character inspired women to imitate her costume. Even a red-spotted fish was named after her. Simon Tappertit, a conceited apprentice at her locksmith father's shop, gave us another term from this novel: *tappertitian*, which refers to a vulgar, showy, and conceited romance.

GRADGRIND

One who is solely interested in cold, hard facts.

Thomas Gradgrind is the utilitarian mill owner in Dickens's novel *Hard Times*. He runs a school where he believes hard facts, rules, and calculations are more important than love, emotions, and feelings. He is converted in the end when his daughter Louisa has an emotional breakdown.

PODSNAP

Someone displaying self-satisfied complacency and an insular attitude.

In *Our Mutual Friend*, Dickens's last completed novel, businessman John Podsnap has a very high opinion of himself. He is wrapped in his own little world: "He never could make out why everybody was not quite satisfied, and he felt conscious that he set a brilliant social example in being particularly well satisfied with most things, and, above all other things, with himself."

It's easy for Podsnap to dismiss unpleasant facts with the wave of his arm: "With his favourite right-arm flourish which sweeps away everything and settles it for ever, Mr Podsnap sweeps these inconveniently unexplainable wretches who have lived beyond their means and gone to total smash, off the face of the universe."

His blindness to others gives him a feeling of superiority. His life, his country, his way are the best: "We Englishmen are Very Proud of our Constitution, Sir. It Was Bestowed Upon Us By Providence. No Other Country is so Favoured as This Country."

In his dystopian novel *Brave New World*, Aldous Huxley called the cloning method used to make thousands of identical "ideal" humans "Podsnap's Technique."

CHADBAND

An unctuous hypocritical person.

Dickens commented on society through his novels and their characters. The Reverend Mr. Chadband in the novel *Bleak House* is one such character. He pretends to be all things spiritual, but the reality is different. He calls himself a "vessel" and if he were one, he would be one oily, greasy vessel. Dickens sets him straight in his portrayal, alluding to his prodigious appetite: "For, Chadband is rather a consuming vessel . . . a gorging vessel."

TURVEYDROP

One who is, or feigns to be, a perfect model of deportment.

Mr. Turveydrop is another character from *Bleak House* who should be the brother of Chadband. He runs a dance academy and presents himself as a beacon of dignity and right behavior. In reality, he's the perfect embodiment of a conceited hypocrite, a self-indulgent man.

36. What's the longest word you can think of that has only one vowel?

PECKSNIFFIAN

Sanctimoniously hypocritical.

It'd be hard to find a name catchier than Pecksniff in literature. Seth Pecksniff is a surveyor and architect in Dickens's novel *Martin Chuzzlewit*. He also teaches architecture, and as one "who has never designed or built anything," he doesn't shy from passing off his students' designs as his own.

Mr. Pecksniff is greedy and deceitful, but that doesn't prevent him from expounding on moral rectitude and piety. He's described this way in the novel: "Some people likened him to a direction-post, which is always telling the way to a place, and never goes there." His two daughters are named Mercy and Charity.

GAMP

A large umbrella.

In the novel *Martin Chuzzlewit*, Mrs. Gamp is a midwife and nurse. She is equally enthusiastic in "layering out" of the dead as in delivering a baby, irrespective of her training (or lack of it). Mrs. Gamp is a fat old woman and she is highspirited, in both senses of the term. She loves to carry a large cotton umbrella. An umbrella is called *gamp* after her name.

The word *umbrella* came from Latin *umbra* (shade). Besides *gamp*, the word *umbrella* has a number of colorful synonyms: *brolly*, which is an alteration of the word *umbrella*; blending the sounds of *umbrella* and *parachute* gave us *bumbershoot*; and *parasol* is derived from Italian *para-* (guarding against) and *sole* (sun).

37. The word *bid* is unique when it comes to reflection. What's special about that word?

SCROOGE

A miser.

Scrooge is perhaps the most famous of all Dickens's characters. Ebenezer Scrooge is the mean-spirited protagonist of *A Christmas Carol*. He epitomizes miserliness. According to his penny-pinching ways, money is his supreme goal in life. He cries out, "Bah, Humbug!" in response to "Happy Christmas" or anything else that doesn't help add to the bottom line.

On Christmas Eve he is visited by the three ghosts, the Ghosts of Christmas Past, Present, and Future, who show him his young life, present life, and the life yet to come. Ultimately, Scrooge is reformed and becomes a charitable, caring, and giving person, but the term *Scrooge* applies to the penny-pinching one.

DICKENS/DICKENSIAN

Dickens's vivid portrayal of Victorian England has turned his name itself into an eponym. The word *Dickensian* refers to a harsh world reminiscent of the Victorian era, a time marked by poor living conditions, grime, exploitation, etc. This is how the *New York Times* describes immigrant workers' conditions in Dubai in a March 2006 article: "Far from the high-rise towers and luxury hotels emblematic of Dubai, the workers turning this swath of desert into a modern metropolis live in a Dickensian world of cramped labor camps, low pay, and increasing desperation."

Use of the word *dickens* in exclamations, as in "What the dickens do you want?" is much older. It has nothing to do with Charles Dickens. It's supposed to be a replacement for "devil." It has been recorded in use more than two hundred years before the birth of the novelist.

~ Chapter 9 ~

Words to Describe
People: Insults

Mark Twain once said, "When angry, count to four; when very angry, swear." While swearing is considered uncouth and vulgar, it has its place and purpose. It helps provide an emotional release and clears the system. Isn't a verbal venting of emotions better than a physical one?

You don't have to rely on those worn-out four-letter terms to inflict rude remarks on the target. With a careful selection of words, it's possible to elevate insults to an art form. Why not use this chapter's exquisite words for one of those times when nothing less will do?

These are words you can safely use to describe your coworkers, associates, and others. Try these elegantly veiled insults without fear of offending, just make sure they don't have a dictionary handy.

But remember, everything in moderation.

OLEAGINOUS

Marked by excessive and false earnestness; ingratiating.

We don't like oily, greasy food. Or people. No wonder there are so many words to describe oily people. Other words that are synonyms of this are *smarmy*, from dialectal smarm (to smear), and *unctuous*, from Latin *unctus* (act of anointing).

We acquired oleaginous from Latin *oleaginus* (of the olive tree), from *olea* (the olive tree).

SAPONACEOUS

Soapy, slippery, evasive.

A *saponaceous* person would be one having the qualities of soap: slippery and smooth, hard to handle. The word originated from Latin *sapon-* (soap).

If an oleaginous person meets with someone saponaceous, do they neutralize each other?

SANSCULOTTE

Any revolutionary with extremist views.

The term is a generalization of the name for extreme radical republicans during the French Revolution. The word is from French, literally, "without knee breeches." In the French Revolution, this was the aristocrats' term of contempt for the ill-clad volunteers of the Revolutionary army, who rejected knee breeches as a symbol of the upper class and adopted pantaloons. As often happens with such epithets, the revolutionaries themselves adopted it as a term of pride.

FUSSBUDGET

One who is fussy about unimportant things.

The word budget is a marvelous example of how language goes around. The French *bougette* (little bag) came to English, developed a new sense—*budget* (a financial estimate)—and then went back to French in its new avatar. Most living languages are mongrels and that's what makes them richer. Why make a fuss about keeping them "pure"?

A few variants of this word are *fussbag*, *fussbucket*, and *fusspot*. Usually we dislike fussbudgets, but sometimes we wish there were fussbudgets among our elected leaders who cared enough to fuss about the nation's budget.

One of the most famous fictional fussbudgets is Lucy in Charles Schulz's comic strip *Peanuts*.

REBARBATIVE

Irritating; repellent.

From Latin *barba* (beard) came *rebarbative*. Are bearded people irritating? While some find a beard on a man attractive, it could be like barbed wire—repelling—for others. In fact, the words *barb*, *barber*, and *beard* are derived from the same Latin root.

ILLEIST

One who refers to oneself in the third person.

We have all seen them: celebrities who step up to the microphone during a press interview and talk about themselves as if they had been talking about a friend, in third person. On being inducted in the Baseball Hall of Fame, Ozzie Smith said, "Ozzie Smith is not a uniquely talented person. In fact, he is no different than any man, woman, boy, or girl in this audience today."

There are many well-known illeists—from cartoon character Elmo to advice columnist Miss Manners to Senator Bob Dole—we find them among real as well as fictional characters.

But for some reason illeism is especially attractive to professional sports players. The award for the best display of illeism has to go to baseball player Rickey Henderson, who left this message on his manager's voice-mail: "Kevin, this is Rickey, calling on behalf of Rickey" (quoted in *Sports Illustrated*).

38. What's the only language name that's a palindrome?

The word originated from Latin *ille* (that).

Then, there is nosism, the practice of referring to oneself in the plural as "we." Because it's often used by editors, it's also known as the "editorial we." It's often called "the royal we" as in Queen Victoria's oft-reported remark "We are not amused."

Mark Twain said upon the practice of nosism, "Only kings, presidents, editors, and people with tapeworms have the right to use the editorial 'we.'"

The word *nosism* comes from Latin *nos*, first-person plural pronoun. The word *us* is from the same source.

Too frequent use of nosism leads to *weism*, also known as *wegotism* (a blend of *we* and *egotism*).

CRITICASTER

An incompetent critic.

Here is a lovely prefix that can come in handy when we need words to put someone down—*aster*. This pejorative suffix, indicating something inferior, small, or shallow, could be applied to almost any noun. A reviewer calls a poet a poetaster (an inferior poet), and the poet might return the favor by calling him a criticaster.

Possibilities are endless: politicaster, musicaster, philosophaster, etc. But let's remember that a grandmaster is not an inferior grandma.

ALITERATE

One who is capable of reading but not interested in it.

Aliterates stand somewhere between literates and illiterates. They can read but don't want to. Whether they can alliterate,

39. Reverse the letters of this English word and it still means the same thing in French. What's the word?

I'm not sure about. Mark Twain probably had aliterates in mind when he said, "The man who doesn't read good books has no advantage over the man who can't read them."

The word is derived from Latin *littera* (letter).

RAMPALLION OR RAMPALLIAN

A ruffian or scoundrel.

In Shakespeare's *Henry IV*, Falstaff exclaims, "Away, you scullion! You rampallion! You fustilarian! I'll tickle your catastrophe." *Scullion* is a kitchen servant or one who does menial work. *Fustilarian* is a synonym of the term *fustilugs* (a fat and slovenly person).

Alas, the origin of rampallian remains elusive.

BLUNDERBUSS

A clumsy, blundering person.

Blunderbuss was a short, wide-mouthed gun used to scatter shots at close range. The gun wasn't known for its precise shot. Its scattershot effect resulted in its name being altered from *donderbus* to *blunderbuss*. It wasn't long before the word was applied to insensitive, blundering persons.

The term derives from the alteration of Dutch *donderbus*, from *donder* (thunder) + *bus* (gun, tube).

* * *

Not to spread too much negativity, here are a few words with positive meanings. Then again, you could use them in insults, too, as in telling someone, "You aren't exactly a polyhistor, are you?"

POLYHISTOR

A person of great or wide learning.

A *polyhistor* is a person with encyclopedic knowledge, and so is a polymath. These two words are perfect synonyms but are really exceptions. There are not a lot of words where you could replace one with another without at least a slight change in the shade of meaning. On the surface, two words may appear similar, but look deeper and you will surely find subtle nuances, each word carrying its own flavor of meaning, as if created to fulfill its destiny where no other word can.

The word came from Greek *polyistor*, from *poly-* (much, many) and *histor* (learned). *Polymath* is from *manthanein* (to learn).

PHILOMATH

A lover of learning.

A *philomath* isn't one who loves mathematics, rather one who is fond of learning. The word is from Greek *philo-* (loving) and *manthanein* (to learn). The word *mathematics* is a special case of the same Greek word *manthanein*. One who learns late in life is known as an *opsimath*, from Greek *opsi-* (late).

RIDENT

Laughing; cheerful.

Rident resulted from Latin *ridere* (to laugh), which is also the source of *ridiculous*, *deride*, and *risible*. Tetanus can cause the muscles of the face to contort into a grinning expression. The condition is known as *risus sardonicus*, or sardonic grin.

DIGLOT

Bilingual.

A *diglot* isn't someone who digs a lot. Nor is it one who digs much, or one who digs a parcel of land. Rather, the term refers to one who is bilingual or speaks two languages. And a diglot book is one that has side-by-side text in two languages, on the same or opposite page.

From digging lots to digging languages—it's quite a stretch.

But that's what happens sometimes when we try to guess the meaning of words. We tend to parse them among familiar boundaries, leading to unusual results.

The word was born after the Greek *di-* (two) married *glossa* (tongue, language).

40. Some sentences make sense only when spoken, not when written. Can you think of any?

~ *Chapter 10* ~

Streets That Became Metaphors

Gritty streets of the real life often turn up as metaphors in our language—at times with contradictions! A *man on the street* is an average person, a *Joe Blow*, not necessarily one with street smarts. And a *woman in the street* is the feminine equivalent, but it's not the same as a *streetwalker*.

Political maneuvering often takes place on the *back street*. Who doesn't wish to reach *Easy Street*? Product marketeers try to appeal to the *main street*, but who cares about the *man on the street*? Human languages never were logical, a reflection of people who created them.

Here are a few more terms that are now part of the English language. At one time these streets, alleys, avenues, and rows were specific places, but as metaphors today they mean much more than a particular address.

GRUB STREET

Collective term for hack writers.

In seventeenth-century London, Grub Street near Moorfields was the place to find impoverished writers. Even though this street was renamed as Milton Street in 1830, the world of hack writers is still known as Grub Street.

The inhabitants of this now metaphorical place churn out words without any regard for their literary merit. They were often called penny-a-liners. A Grub Street writer is also called a hack writer, which is another London allusion: Hackney in East London was the place where horses suitable for routine riding or driving were raised. The word *hack*, in related senses, is a short form of *hackney*.

Samuel Johnson in his famous dictionary described *Grub Street* as "much inhabited by writers of small histories, dictionaries, and temporary poems."

What does a writer on Grub Street write? Potboilers, of course!

FLEET STREET

British press considered collectively.

At one time Fleet Street in London was the center of English journalism. Even though all the news agencies have left the street for other locations, its name continues to be synonymous with the British newspaper industry. In June 2005, Reuters became the last agency to say good-bye to the street.

Fleet Street is nicknamed "The Street of Shame" for the gossip printed by British tabloids.

WALL STREET

The center of the U.S. financial world.

Named after a street in lower Manhattan in New York City, which was once home to most of the major investment firms, banks, financial analysts, and the New York Stock Exchange. The street got its name from the defensive wall that Dutch

41. What's the word with the greatest number of silent letters?

colonists built in 1653 to protect the area from attacks by British troops and Native Americans.

Counterparts of Wall Street in other countries are Bay Street (Toronto, Canada), Dalal Street (Mumbai, India), and The City or The Square Mile (London, UK).

MADISON AVENUE

Advertising industry in the United States.

The term is coined after Madison Avenue, a street in New York City that was once the center of the U.S. advertising industry. But where did the street get its name from? From the place where it starts—Madison Square. And why was Madison Square called Madison Square? It was named in honor of James Madison, fourth president of the United States.

Who would have thought Madison, this shy, serious, short man (at 5 feet 4 inches, or 1.62 meters, the shortest president in U.S. history), would one day have his name tacked to the industry noted for its bombast and tall tales?

And where did James Madison get his name from? Of course, from his dad, Colonel James Madison, Sr. The name Madison indicated a son of Madde, Maud, Madeleine, or Matthew. These days, it's a popular name for both boys and girls.

The glitzy, insincere, and often deceptive practices of the advertising and public relations industries have resulted in this term often used to describe something less than truthful. Perhaps it's symbolic that Park Avenue—a street synonymous with luxury, fashion, affluence, and high living—runs parallel to Madison Avenue.

TIN PAN ALLEY

Popular-music industry; composers, songwriters, and music publishers considered collectively. The term is pejorative, and is perhaps the musical equivalent of Grub Street.

The term gets its name after West 28th Street in New York City, once the home of America's most important music publishers. From the cacophony of cheap pianos and hack musicians, the area came to be known as Tin Pan Alley (apparently *Tin Pan* was slang for *tinny piano*) and eventually became generalized to refer to the whole music industry. The term, popular in the past, is less used today.

The corresponding British term is *Denmark Street* in London.

This kind of allusion is an example of synecdoche, a figure of speech where part is used for the whole or vice versa.

Some idioms involving the word *alley* are *back alley* (underhanded), *blind alley* (hopeless), and *up your alley* (suitable with one's interests or abilities). Only in a human language could *up your alley* and *down your alley* mean the same thing.

SKID ROW

A run-down part of a town inhabited by vagrants and alcoholics.

The origin of the term is in the Pacific Northwest. Yesler Way in Seattle claims to be the first skid row. This sloping road was used by the loggers to slide logs down to the lumber mills. The area was frequented by loggers who congregated in the cheap bars after work. This skid road turned into Skid Row.

Just north of Seattle, the Canadian city of Vancouver saw a parallel evolution of skid row. Today there are skid rows in many towns, and the idiom *on the skids* means in the process of decline.

MAIN STREET

A place that represents provincialism, mediocrity, and complacency.

In 1920 Sinclair Lewis published his novel *Main Street*,

which shattered the idealized image of small-town America. His novel showed the parochial outlook of a town inhabited by self-complacent residents uninterested in anything outside their limited world. The story takes place in the fictional town of Gopher Prairie, Minnesota, where the female protagonist tries in vain to interest her fellow townspeople in reform.

Lewis peered beneath the mythologized small-town life and showed that below its nostalgic layers lay indifference, narrow-mindedness, and materialism. No wonder most politicians try to appeal to Main Street.

In Britain, *Acacia Avenue* is the term for middle-class values.

EASY STREET

A state of financial security.

If you are on *easy street*, you're living a comfortable life, financially speaking. The term is self-descriptive. Easy street isn't uphill. We just hope you didn't reach easy street with easy money.

PRIMROSE PATH

A life of pleasure and ease.

A *primrose path* is one devoted to pleasure, especially sensual pleasure. It could also refer to a path that looks promising but leads to disaster. A primrose is one of various plants, typically with yellow flowers. The word *primrose* is from Latin *prima rosa* (first rose) but why primrose path? Shakespeare coined the metaphor and probably alliteration influenced the selection of primroses. It could very well have been rose road or azalea avenue or buttercup boulevard instead.

42. *What U.S. states are named in Spanish?*

The first occurrence of the term is in Shakespeare's *Hamlet*, where Ophelia rebuffs her brother Laertes' advice with:

Do not, as some ungracious pastors do,
Show me the steep and thorny way to Heaven,
Whilst, like a puff'd and reckless libertine,
Himself the primrose path of dalliance treads
And recks not his own rede [heeds not his own counsel].

Shakespeare used the metaphor later in *Macbeth* as well.

* * *

Before we move on, let's take a moment to see where these various terms for passageways came from:

Alley came from French *aller* (to go).
Avenue is literally a *venue*, from French *venir* (to come).
Boulevard came to English via French, Dutch, and German,
    meaning a rampart converted into a promenade.
Road was a place where one rode.
Row was a road formed by a row of buildings.
And *street* derived from Latin *sternere* (to stretch or spread).

43. *What's the shortest everyday word in which each vowel is used once and only once?*

~ *Chapter 11* ~

How Do You Measure the Warmth of Clothes?

In Tolstoy's story "How Much Land Does a Man Need?" Pahom, a peasant, goes to buy land from the Bashkirs. He asks the sellers the price, and they quote him a thousand rubles a day. Pahom is surprised at this unusual rate. When he asks how many acres that would be, they reply that they do not understand acres. Pahom could get as much land as he could cover in a day—by walking on it.

Pahom starts early, walking all day under the hot sun, without rest, hoping to cover a big area. . . . If only the Bashkirs knew their acres and feet, poor Pahom wouldn't have met his tragic end (but then we wouldn't have a parable on the man's greed).

Ancient measurements were based on the human body. A *foot* was as long as the length of the foot of an average human (or the King, according to some). Same with the *hand* (four inches), which is still the unit to measure the height of a horse. A *cubit* was the length of the forearm, from the elbow to the tip of the middle finger. A *pace* was the length of a single step. A *furlong* came from *furrow long*, alluding to the plowing of land; a furlong was equal to a stadium, one-eighth of a Roman mile. Today when building a stadium, we don't have to limit it to a "stadium" length.

We've come a long way from those ancient units, though we still continue to use some of the old terms like *foot*. And often informal units work even better than meters or feet. To say that "every year more than sixty Rhode Islands of rainforests are chopped down" gives a more vivid picture. Wales is the UK equivalent of the Rhode Island measure.

Here are some of the more unusual units and the stories behind them.

DOL

Dol is a unit of the intensity of pain.

How do you measure something as subjective as pain? One person might say, "My head is bursting"; another might say, "My head is killing me." Whose head is giving more trouble?

Three Cornell University researchers, James Hardy, Herbert Wolff, and Helen Goodell, experimented by radiating heat on volunteers' heads and foreheads. They came up with a unit of pain they called a dol (from Latin *dolor*, "pain") and theorized that one dol is equivalent to two *jnd*, or "just noticeable difference." There is also the dolorimeter, an instrument for measuring pain.

The same Latin root *dolor*, which was the source of *dol*, has given us words like *condole*, *dolor*, and *indolent*. Then there is the Greek root *algo-*, meaning "pain." There are algometers, which measure pain by applying pressure.

Usually having a phobia might brand you as a nut, but here is a phobia that indicates you're a regular human being if you have it: *algophobia*. It's the fear of pain. The word indicates an unusual, morbid fear of pain, producing intense anxiety.

Now for a few unrelated *algo* words. *Algology* has nothing to do with pain. It's the study of algae. It's also known as phycology. And *algorithm* came from the name of a ninth-century Muslim mathematician of Persian origin, al-Khwarizmi. Just how many dols the study of algae or algorithms results in, we're not sure.

TOG

A *tog* defines how warm a cloth can keep you. It's the unit of thermal insulation of clothing. The name of this unit takes us back to ancient Rome, where citizens wore a loose outer garment—a toga—in public.

A light cotton T-shirt would be rated about one tog. About ten togs is the thickest clothing that's still practical to wear, but you don't have to limit yourself to the number of togs in a comforter. On the other hand, it's the air that works as an insulator, so when you buy a thick comforter, you're essentially paying for air.

The instrument to measure the warmth of clothes is called a togmeter. Now, if only there were one to measure the warmth of the wearers!

The word *tog* is mostly used in Europe. In the United States the unit used is *clo* (shortening of *clothes*). A clo is defined as the insulation needed to keep a sitting, resting person warm in a room at 70 degrees Fahrenheit. A clo is equal to approximately one and a half togs.

As if color, size, and style weren't enough things to look for when shopping for clothes, now we have clos and togs. Next time you happen to be at Macy's, try this, "I'm looking for a nice jacket in a shade of burgundy in, say, about two clos or a tog rating of three."

44. What U.S. state is named in French?

HEMIDEMISEMIQUAVER

This British term for a musical note sounds more musical than its prosaic American equivalent "sixty-fourth note," but it's a long word to describe a short note (⅛ of a quaver, or 1/64 of a whole note).

Notes even smaller than this are possible though not very common. In this word we've made use of all the prefixes for the sense *half*: Greek *hemi-*, Latin *semi-*, and French *demi-*. It's time to start repeating them: semihemidemisemiquaver is 1/128 of a whole note. Quasihemidemisemiquaver is also seen, from Latin *quasi-* (meaning "resembling," literally "as if").

But why single out hemidemisemiquaver for being a long word to describe a short note. After all, the word *monosyllable* has five syllables in it.

BARN

10^{-28} 10^{-24}

A *barn* is a unit for the cross section of the nucleus of an atom. 1 barn $= 10^{28}$ square meters. The unit is whimsically named after the expression "as big as a barn," since atomic dimensions are so tiny. Who says nuclear physicists don't have a sense of humor?

MILLIHELEN

It's a facetious unit of beauty. It's the amount of beauty needed to launch one ship. Helen of Troy, whose abduction resulted in the Trojan War, caused the launch of a thousand ships. In Christopher Marlowe's *The Tragical History of Doctor Faustus*, Faustus says to Helen, "Was this the face that launch'd a thousand ships?"

Variations of this unit are possible. Assuming there are one

45. How are legislators like allegorists?

hundred sailors in a ship, ten microhelens might be the beauty required to motivate one sailor. We could even go negative: a unit of ugliness might be a negative millihelen: one that's needed to sink one ship.

THERBLIG

Many units are named after inventors: newton, curie, ampere, henry, joule, bel—are all units named to honor the people who did groundbreaking research in the field. Sometimes unit names are coined after reversing the names.

A *therblig* is a unit of work (or the absence of it) in an industrial operation. It's named after engineer Frank Bunker Gilbreth (1868–1924), who did pioneering work in time-and-motion studies. Gilbreth divided an operation into sixteen standardized activities, later expanded to eighteen. These are: search, find, select, grasp, hold, position, assemble, use, disassemble, inspect, transport loaded, transport unloaded, preposition for next operation, release load, unavoidable delay, avoidable delay, plan, and rest for overcoming fatigue. (In modern times, he might have added "surfing the Web" as well.)

Gilbreth called these fundamental elements of a task therbligs, a reverse of his name (with *th* considered a single unit). His study into human movement and its efficiency was not limited to just the shop floor. He went as far as studying surgical operations. He and his wife, Lillian Moller Gilbreth, had twelve children, and the whole clan helped with the research. They often employed their children as guinea pigs to study motion.

His son Frank Jr. and daughter Ernestine detailed their adventures in a 1948 book titled *Cheaper by the Dozen*, which was turned into a (what else?) *motion* picture in 1950 (a second version was released in 2003).

MHO

Mho is a unit of electrical conductance. Conductance tells how easily current flows in a material. The name of the unit mho was coined by reversing ohm, the unit of electrical resistance. Both mho and ohm are named after German physicist Georg Simon Ohm (1789–1854).

Now mho has been replaced by *siemens*, named after another German engineer, Werner von Siemens (1816–1892). Mho is quite different from IMHO, a common abbreviation for "In My Humble Opinion."

LIGHT YEAR

What a misleading name for a unit! It sounds like this would be the unit of time, but a *light year* is a measure of distance. It's how far light would travel in a year. That's nearly 6 trillion miles. Think how many frequent-flier miles light would collect if it chose to ride in an airline. Another astronomical unit of distance that looks like a unit of time is *parsec* (from parallax second). One parsec is equal to 3.26 light years.

The idea of talking about distance in terms of time isn't all that unusual. We do it all the time. Portland is about three hours from Seattle, we might say, the assumption being that one is driving in a car at an average speed of sixty miles an hour.

MINER'S INCH

Now here is one that appears to be a unit of distance, but it really measures water flow. A *miner's inch* is how much water flows in a minute from an opening one inch across and one inch high. The actual unit varies from place to place, since the flow depends on the water pressure, but it's around 1.5 cubic feet per minute. A similar unit is known as a *water inch*. Another is an *acre foot*, a unit of volume.

Extreme Prefixes and Suffixes

For our daily life, miles and kilometers are good enough. But when we talk about astronomical or atomic distances, we have to go beyond them. Here are the standard prefixes designated by the International System of Units. As these origins show, scientists are not afraid to have a little fun when it comes to nomenclature. Look for the origin of *tera* or *nano* below, for example.

Factor	Prefix	Symbol	Origin
10^{24}	yotta	Y	Greek *okto* (eight)
10^{21}	zetta	Z	Latin *septem* (seven)
10^{18}	exa	E	Greek *sex* (six)
10^{15}	peta	P	Greek *pente* (five)
10^{12}	tera	T	Greek *tera* (monster), similar to *tetra* (four)
10^{9}	giga	G	Greek *gigas* (giant)
10^{6}	mega	M	Greek *megas* (great)
10^{3}	kilo	k	Greek *chilioi* (thousand)
10^{2}	hecto	h	Greek *hecaton* (hundred)
10^{1}	deca	da	Greek *deka* (ten)
10^{0}	one		
10^{-1}	deci	d	Latin *decimus* (tenth)
10^{-2}	centi	c	Latin *centum* (hundred)
10^{-3}	milli	m	Latin *mille* (thousand)
10^{-6}	micro	μ	Greek *mikros* (small)
10^{-9}	nano	n	Greek *nanos* (dwarf)

46. *"Show this bold Prussian that brings slaughter, slaughter brings rout!" This sentence can turn into another perfectly sensible sentence with removal of a letter from each word. What is it?*

10^{-12}	pico	p	Spanish *pico* (beak, peak, bit)
10^{-15}	femto	f	Danish or Norwegian *femten* (fifteen)
10^{-18}	atto	a	Danish or Norwegian *atten* (eighteen)
10^{-21}	zepto	z	Latin *septem* (seven)
10^{-24}	yocto	y	Greek *okto* (eight)

There is plenty of scope to use these prefixes in our day-to-day life. While on the phone, instead of saying, "Hold on for a moment," try "Hold on for a nanocentury!" That's only three seconds! Many professors believe that the ideal duration of a lecture is one microcentury: about fifty-three minutes.

Why not beyond yotta? Because the radius of the observable universe is not more than a few yottameters. On the other side of the scale, the mass of a proton or neutron is 1.6 yg (yoctogram). These prefixes are good enough even to describe Bill Gates's fortune. But if you need to go further, there is always googolplex (1 followed by googol zeros). Then there are the informal zillion and even bigger gazillion. These are jocular alterations of million or billion.

And there is, maybe, even a bigger one. The story goes that George W. Bush is informed that three Brazilian soldiers had died in a bomb attack in Iraq. He is visibly perturbed. Later, he asks, "How many is a brazillian?"

Scientists have stopped at 10^{24} and 10^{-24} but there are English names for these numbers and beyond. A centillion is one followed by 303 zeros.

Nobel Prize–winning physicist Richard Feynman once said,

47. *What synthetic fiber was named by anagramming the word expands?*

"There are 10^{11} stars in the galaxy. That used to be a huge number. But it's only a hundred billion. It's less than the national deficit! We used to call them astronomical numbers. Now we should call them economical numbers."

Scales and Scores

We all are familiar with the Richter scale, which tells us about the severity of an earthquake. There are scales to measure almost everything under the sun. There's one about the risk of a wayward asteroid hitting the earth, one about the intensity of hurricanes, and even one about the health of a baby just brought by the stork.

TORINO SCALE

The evening news mentions a new asteroid discovered in Earth's orbit and the possibility that it might collide with our planet. What are you going to do? Is it time to start repenting for your sins?

The *Torino scale* presents an objective measure of the probability of an asteroid or comet hitting the earth and causing damage. It's a scale in a 0–10 range that assigns value to the heavenly objects by factoring in their mass, velocity, and the probability of reaching Earth.

It was devised in 1999 at a meeting in Turin, Italy. On this scale, a 0 means virtually no chance of collision (continue eating your dinner in peace), while a 10 means certain catastrophe on a global scale (time to pray).

The highest level ever given on the Torino scale was a 4 in December 2004. It was for an asteroid with a 2 percent chance of hitting Earth in 2029. Thankfully, after further observation, it was later downgraded to a 2 on the Torino scale.

No fear—astronomers who came up with the scale say that a

planetary object must be at 8 on the Torino scale before there's any certainty of it hitting Earth and causing destruction in even a limited area. Just in case you're curious, here's what the scale says for the level 10: "A collision is certain, capable of causing global climatic catastrophe that may threaten the future of civilization as we know it, whether impacting land or ocean. Such events occur on average once per 100,000 years, or less often."

Now at least movie producers have more scientific ways of presenting facts in their thrillers. The Torino scale is meant to convey the degree of risk to the lay public and assuage fears so we know all asteroids are not out Turin the earth. Astronomers use a more specialized scale known as the Palermo scale for their own purposes. What is it that makes astronomers meet in Italy to come up with these scales?

SAFFIR-SIMPSON HURRICANE SCALE

It's a scale to assess potential damage and flooding that a hurricane would cause upon landfall. It was created in 1969 by consulting engineer Herbert Saffir and Bob Simpson, then director of the U.S. National Hurricane Center. The scale ranges from 1 to 5: A category 1 hurricane would damage unanchored mobile homes, while a category 5 is one in which one could imagine cows flying.

There's also the Fujita scale, devised by meteorologist T. Theodore Fujita, for estimating tornado damage after a tornado has passed an area. It goes from category F0 to F6. If things are not so extreme, one would employ the Beaufort Wind scale, created by Sir Francis Beaufort of the British Navy. It's used simply for estimating wind speeds.

APGAR SCORE

A method of assessing a newborn baby's health.

This is a judging world. We're evaluated right from birth

(Apgar score) to death (how many people came to the funeral). In 1953 anesthesiologist Dr. Virginia Apgar (1909–1974) devised a quick way to measure the health of a newborn child. She assigned 0, 1, or 2 points for each of the five criteria: heart rate, respiration, muscle tone, skin color, and reflex response. The Apgar score is typically calculated at one minute and five minutes after birth. Ten years after the debut of the Apgar score, Dr. L. Joseph Butterfield introduced an acronym as a mnemonic aid for the term: Appearance, Pulse, Grimace, Activity, Respiration.

The image that comes to mind is that of the Winter Olympics and a competition that's a cross between the bobsled and figure skiing. The newborn comes sliding down and there's this team of judges—doctors and nurses—holding up cards with the points they awarded. Many a parent has now one more number to boast of, besides the usual weight and height, for their newborn.

Time

The wheel of time keeps moving. The old year drifts away and the new year claims its place. There's a reason we call it the "wheel" of time. The word *annual* comes from the Latin *annus*, meaning a circuit of the sun, hence a year. Here are the terms for various anniversaries:

2nd   biennial, also diennial
3rd   triennial
4th   quadrennial, also quadriennial

48. *What's common among the words* escalator, celluloid, *and* cornflakes?

5th	quinquennial
6th	sexennial
7th	septennial
8th	octennial
9th	novennial
10th	decennial
11th	undecennial
12th	duodecennial
13th	tridecennial
15th	quindecennial
17th	septendecennial
20th	vicennial, also vigentennial
40th	quadragennial
50th	semicentennial or quinquagennial
100th	centennial
125th	quasquicentennial
150th	sesquicentennial
200th	bicentennial
300th	tercentennial, also tricentennial
400th	quadricentennial, also quatercentennial
500th	quincentennial
600th	sexcentennial
700th	septcentennial
800th	octocentennial
1000th	millennial

And finally, *forever* would be perennial.

---

49. These two three-letter words are pronounced exactly the same, yet have no letters in common. What are they?

~ *Chapter 12* ~

Places That Became Words

Once upon a time, a person's name was his complete business card. It could comprise his given name, profession, father's or mother's name, a personal trait, and the name of his village. That was because where one lived, more than anything else, defined a person.

The place of origin often turned into a generic term for some personal characteristic. The English language embraces many words that were coined when a place had become linked with a particular quality.

Soloi, an ancient Athenian colony in Cilicia, was one of those places. Because its colonists spoke a dialect considered substandard, the place came to be forever associated with errors. The result was the term *solecism*: an error or impropriety, such as a grammatical mistake or a breach of etiquette.

Thankfully, we don't have to include our location or profession anymore. I certainly wouldn't have wanted to change my name each of the three times I've moved in the last ten years.

A word resulting from the generalization of a place name is called a toponym, from the Greek *topo* (place) + *-onym* (name). Let's look at a few of these words.

Greek Places That Became Words

LACONIC

Someone *laconic* is a person known for speaking few words. The idea behind the term is best illustrated by the people after whom the word is coined: the residents of Laconia, an ancient country in southern Greece (capital: Sparta). The story goes that Philip of Macedon threatened Laconians by saying that if he entered Laconia, he'd raze Sparta to the ground. To this, the Laconians simply replied, "If." Well aware of their discipline (see Spartan below) and bravery, Philip wisely left them alone.

Not a bad way to ward off an attack, though one has to wonder where they got their talk-show hosts from.

Speaking of laconic people, Calvin Coolidge, thirtieth president of the United States, was famous for his stinginess with words. Once, a woman approached him and told him that she had bet that she could get more than two words out of him. Silent Cal replied, "You lose."

North Carolina has a newspaper called the *Standard Laconic*. I wonder if it's a single-sheet newspaper.

SPARTAN

The term *spartan* signifies something or someone who is self-restrained, frugal, or brave.

It seems Laconians, especially those in the capital city of Sparta, were parsimonious not just with words, but in their whole approach to life. Their lives were marked by austerity, discipline, courage, and bravery.

Spartans placed high importance on simplicity and self-restraint. Well, maybe that's because they didn't have a Shopping Channel.

The Greek historian Thucydides (c.460–c.400 BCE) wrote, "Suppose the city of Sparta to be deserted, and nothing left but the temples and the ground-plan, distant ages would be very unwilling to believe that the power of the Laconians was at all equal to their fame." One doesn't need to have material things to be famous. All that's needed is to encourage people to coin words after oneself.

SYBARITE

A *sybarite* is someone devoted to the life of luxury and sensual pleasure. We got the term from the residents of Sybaris, an ancient Greek colony in southern Italy.

Even though Sybarites and Spartans weren't that far apart geographically, metaphorically speaking they could have been poles apart. Sybaris was in a fertile region. It was noted for its wealth and splendor, and its citizens had developed a well-deserved reputation for sensual gratification and indulgence.

This voluptuousness was their downfall. Sybarites had even taught their horses to dance to lively tunes. When a nearby city named Croton attacked Sybaris, the crafty Crotons didn't bring out their best armaments. Rather, they led with their finest musicians playing lively tunes on their pipes. When the Sybarite cavalry came charging, their horses paid more attention to the music than to the soldiers mounted upon them. The horses danced, the Sybarite army was routed, and the city of Sybaris was destroyed forever. The pipers were hoarse but the horses were piped.

BOEOTIAN

Dull or boorish.

We can thank the people of Boeotia, a district in ancient

50. What country's former and present capital cities are anagrams of each other?

Greece, for this word. Mudslinging isn't something new. Athenians didn't think their neighboring Boeotians were as bright and refined as they themselves were. Since then, the people of Boeotia, which included great men such as Pindar, have forever been maligned in English-language dictionaries.

Today if we needed inspiration to coin a term for boorish behavior, we could just look at pro wrestling.

CORINTHIAN

The profligacy of the natives of Corinth, one of the richest and most powerful cities in ancient Greece, gave us the adjective *corinthian*. When talking about a thing, the word *corinthian* might mean luxurious, but when relating to humans it implies licentious.

It's also the name of one of the five classical orders of building designs (the others are Doric, Ionic, Tuscan, and Composite). In architecture, it tells how to arrange columns and entablature.

Toponyms Related to War (and Peace)
DUNKIRK

A desperate evacuation or retreat; also a crisis requiring drastic measures to avoid total disaster.

The term immortalizes Dunkirk, a seaport and town in northern France. In World War II it was the site of the evacuation of more than 330,000 Allied troops by sea while under German fire during May–June 1940.

It was this Dunkirk that sparked Winston Churchill's

51. What do biplanes *have in common with* jackpots *and* captions?

famous speech in which he declared "Wars are not won by evacuations." Addressing the House of Commons on June 4, 1940, he said, "We shall fight on the beaches, we shall fight on the landing grounds, we shall fight in the fields, and in the streets, we shall fight in the hills; we shall never surrender!"

RUBICON

A point of no return, one where an action taken commits a person irrevocably.

Contrary to popular belief, Caesar salad is not named after Julius Caesar. But the term *Rubicon* does have a connection to him. In 49 BCE, Caesar crossed the Rubicon, a small river that formed the boundary between Cisalpine Gaul and Italy. While doing so, he is reported to have exclaimed *"iacta alea est"* (the die is cast), knowing well that his action signified a declaration of war with Pompeii.

Today when an action marks a situation where there is no going back, we say the Rubicon has been crossed: Once Frumpus signed on the dotted line for the timeshare contract, he realized that he had crossed the Rubicon.

WATERLOO

A crushing or final defeat.

The Battle of Waterloo in 1815 was Napoléon Bonaparte's last battle. He was soundly defeated by the British and Prussian forces, and exiled to the island of Saint Helena. Today the term is used in the phrase "to meet one's Waterloo."

PAX ROMANA

An uneasy peace, especially one imposed by a powerful state on a weaker or vanquished state.

This Latin term literally means "Roman peace," referring to the state of peace during the life of the Roman Empire.

The idea of pax romana is vividly illustrated in *The Life of Gnaeus Julius Agricola*, by the Roman historian Publius Cornelius Tacitus (translated by Alfred John Church and William Jackson Brodribb) when Galgacusk, a British leader, says, "To robbery, slaughter, plunder, they give the lying name of empire; they make a solitude and call it peace."

* * *

Here are a few other toponyms from around the world:

CANOSSA

A place of humiliation or penance. Mostly used in the form "go to Canossa": to humble or humiliate oneself, to eat humble pie.

Government is a good thing, mostly. Religion is perhaps a good thing, too, most of the time. But when the two mix, it's a recipe for disaster (from Latin *dis-+-aster*, literally "unfavorable star").

The story of Canossa is a small slice of the long history of such mix-ups. The metaphorical sense of this term Canossa comes from the name of a ruined castle in the village of Canossa. It was the site of penance by Holy Roman Emperor Henry IV before Pope Gregory VII in January 1077 for calling him a false monk.

The emperor crossed the Alps in the middle of winter to see the pope, who was a guest of Matilda, Countess of Tuscany, at the castle. It's said that Henry stood barefoot in snow outside the castle for three days. That incident later inspired the German chancellor Bismarck to coin the phrase "*Nach Canossa gehen wir nicht*" (We're not going to Canossa) during Kulturkampf.

KILKENNY CATS

People who fight relentlessly till their end.

From a pair of proverbial cats in Kilkenny, Ireland, who

fought till only their tails (or their tales!) were left. According to a story, some people in the town of Kilkenny in Ireland enjoyed tying the tails of two cats and watching them fight till only their tails were left behind. Most likely the story is a parable of a contest between Kilkenny and Irishtown, two municipalities that fought about their boundaries till little more than their tales were left.

Here is a popular limerick (another word that takes its origins from the name of an Irish town) about the cats:

There wanst was two cats of Kilkenny
Each thought there was one cat too many
So they fought and they fit
And they scratched and they bit
'Til instead of two cats there weren't any.

NEANDERTHAL, ALSO NEANDERTAL

Boorish, uncivilized.

The term refers to the Neanderthal man, a member of an extinct subspecies of *Homo sapiens* who lived in caves in Europe and the Mediterranean 200,000 to 30,000 years ago. The name came from Neanderthal (literally, Neander Valley) in western Germany near Düsseldorf, where bones of a Neanderthal man were first discovered in 1856. In 1904 German spelling was regularized, and Thal became Tal.

As an illustration of how convoluted word origins can be, the valley was named after a priest and writer, Joachim Neumann, who chose the pen name of Joachim Neander—he di-

52. Anagrams are words formed by rearranging letters (for example, three turns into ether). Can you form a mathematical expression that remains true even after anagramming?

rectly translated his German last name, Neumann, or "new man," into Greek to form Neander.

The valley was named in honor of Joachim, but today it would be the ultimate insult to call a man Neanderthal. It's also ironic that a term literally meaning "new man" really means a prehistoric man.

MACEDOINE

A mixture of diced fruits or vegetables, often served as a salad, appetizer, or dessert. Also, any medley or mixture.

Macedoine is the French spelling of Macedonia. But why is a mixture of various things called macedoine? The term is apparently an allusion to the diversity of people in the region. Here's how the writer Margo Miller described various art movements in a *Boston Globe* article: "There are similar impulses in Art Nouveau Bing, the English Aesthetic and American Arts and Crafts movements, the Vienna Secession—and the style moderne of Czarist Russia, which mixed them all together in a macedoine."

* * *

And now a few fictional places that have come alive in human imagination and become toponyms:

RURITANIAN

Having the characteristics of some mythical romantic place.

Ruritania was the fictional kingdom in Anthony Hope's 1894 novel *Prisoner of Zenda*. The novel was so successful that Hope brought out two more novels in the same setting. Theater productions and a movie adaptation followed. Eventually

53. What country in the former Yugoslavia gave its name to a type of neckwear?

this spawned a whole new subgenre known as Ruritanian Romance. Even Churchill wrote one, titled *Savrola: A Tale of the Revolution in Laurania*, published in 1900.

STEPFORD

Robotic, compliant, submissive; lacking in individuality.

After the fictional suburb of Stepford, Connecticut, in Ira Levin's 1972 novel, *The Stepford Wives*, later made into movies (in 1975 and 2004). In the story, men of this seemingly ideal town have replaced their wives with attractive robotic dolls devoid of emotion or thought.

XANADU

An idyllic, exotic place of great luxury.

"In Xanadu did Kubla Khan / A stately pleasure-dome decree." These opening lines of Samuel Taylor Coleridge's opium-induced poem *Kubla Khan* brought the word *Xanadu* into common currency in the English language. But the real provenance of Xanadu is Xandu (seventeenth-century spelling, modern spelling Shang-tu), the summer home of Kublai Khan.

Marco Polo's travels to the East and his lofty accounts of Kublai Khan's kingdom forever marked Xanadu as a place of exotic luxury and magnificence.

BRIGADOON

An idyllic place that is out of touch with reality or one that makes its appearance for a brief period in a long time.

From Brigadoon, a village in the 1947 musical of the same name, by Alan Jay Lerner and Frederick Loewe, based on the story *Germelshausen* by Friedrich Gerstacker. Brigadoon is under a spell that makes it invisible to outsiders except on one day every one hundred years.

* * *

Many cities are immortalized in toponymic terms. Here are a few:

PHILADELPHIA LAWYER

A shrewd lawyer, one who is adept at exploiting legal technicalities.

The term *Philadelphia lawyer* can have either positive or negative connotations, depending on whether it's being applied to a lawyer who's for us or against us.

The term can also be applied to a person, not necessarily a lawyer, who is good at manipulating and obfuscating matters.

The most famous Philadelphia lawyer was Andrew Hamilton, who defended John Peter Zenger, printer and publisher of the *New York Weekly Journal*, in a 1735 libel case that set the precedent for free speech in America.

STOCKHOLM SYNDROME

A hostage's attachment to the captor.

Stockholm syndrome is a phenomenon in which hostages begin to identify with and grow sympathetic to their captors. The term is coined after Stockholm, Sweden, the site of a bank robbery.

Consider the Stockholm syndrome if you have any doubt about the veracity of the saying, "Fact is stranger than fiction." In 1973, following a botched robbery attempt, the perpetrator held four employees of a Stockholm bank hostage in the bank vault.

At the end of the five-day captivity, police were surprised to discover that the hostages were afraid of them and resisted rescue. They had bonded with the robber (a prison escapee) and became sympathetic with him. Later, they started a defense fund for him, testified in his favor. One of the female hostages became so bonded to her captor that she continued seeing him after he was imprisoned.

Of course, this phenomenon is not limited to the Swedes. Patty Hearst, heiress to the Hearst publishing fortune, was kidnapped in 1974 by the Symbionese Liberation Army. She later joined her abductors and participated in a bank robbery with them.

More recently, in 2000, an Indian Airlines flight was hijacked and diverted to Kandahar in Afghanistan. The passengers were holed up in the plane for more than a week. At the conclusion of the drama, some passengers were heard saying about the hijackers, "They were not bad people."

Why do people turn around and begin to sympathize with their tormentors in situations like these? It is one of the mysteries of the way the human mind works. Perhaps it is a way for people to cope with the immense immediate stress of being in a situation where their lives depend on their captors.

If one threatens to shoot, and then doesn't, hasn't he done a favor to us, the mind apparently rationalizes. In a place devoid of external contact, the view of reality becomes distorted, and the victims may develop a fondness for the person with the power of life and death over them.

NEW YORK MINUTE
A very short period of time; an instant.

The term alluded to the frenzied pace of life in New York City. New Yorkers are stereotyped as people always in a hurry and often rude, although there are many polite and generous New Yorkers. The term *New York minute* has been facetiously defined as the time between a New York City traffic light's

54. *What's the longest word you can find without ascenders and descenders (that is, with no letters sticking up like* b *or sticking down like* q*)?*

turning green and the driver of the car behind you honking his or her horn.

BOSTON MARRIAGE

A long-term, intimate friendship between two women, often sharing a household.

After Boston (and other areas in the Northeast United States) where such arrangements occurred during the nineteenth century. Perhaps popularized by Henry James's 1886 novel *The Bostonians*, which portrayed such relationships.

ROMAN HOLIDAY

An entertainment event where pleasure is derived from watching gore and barbarism.

From the gladiatorial contests held in ancient Rome. One famous site of such contest was the Colosseum, an amphitheater in Rome completed c. AD 80. Its name is derived from the huge 130-foot colossus of Nero that once stood nearby. The Colosseum was the site of gory gladiatorial contests from which came the term Roman holiday. There were contests between men (slaves and condemned criminals), between man and beast, and between beasts. So much blood flowed, it was said, that after the contest perfume was sprinkled over the audience to mask the stench.

DOOLALLY

Irrational, deranged, or insane.

Deolali, a small town in western India (about 100 miles from Mumbai) has an unusual claim to fame. It's where British

55. What's the only state in the United States with a capital that doesn't share any letters with the name of the state?

soldiers who had completed their tour of duty during the Raj were sent to await transportation home. It was a long wait—often many months—before they were picked up by ships to take them to England. Consequent boredom and heat turned many a soldier insane, and the word *doolally* was coined.

At first the term was used in the form "He's got the Doo-lally tap," from Sanskrit *tapa* (heat) meaning he has caught doolally fever (think an exotic cabin fever), but now it's mostly seen as in "to go doolally." In Australia, it goes as "Don't do your lolly."

An article in the *Economist* (February 21, 2002) described Zimbabwe under Robert Mugabe's rule: "As aid dwindled, Mr Mugabe made no effort to spend within his means. From 1997, public finances went doolally. The main result was graft."

ROSETTA STONE

A clue or key that helps in understanding a previously un-solvable puzzle.

To unravel the origin of this term we have to travel to Egypt. The Rosetta stone is a granite stone tablet (painted black) that was found in 1799 near Rosetta, a town in northern Egypt in the Nile River Delta. It's now in the British Museum and bears the same message written in two languages (Egyptian and Greek), using three different scripts (hieroglyphic, demotic, and Greek).

Discovery of this tablet from 196 BCE, showing the same mes-sage in multiple languages and scripts, made it possible to translate ancient Egyptian hieroglyphs. Nowadays any clue or discovery that helps solve a puzzle or problem is called a Rosetta stone.

GHETTO

Part of a city, typically densely populated and run-down, inhabited by members of an ethnic group or a minority, for social, economic, or legal reasons.

From a word for a foundry, to the name of an island, to the place where Jews were forced to live, to its current sense, the word *ghetto* is a fascinating example of how words come to mean something entirely different as they travel through time. The word originated from Latin *jacere* (to throw), the root of words such as *project*, *inject*, *adjective*, and *jet*.

In Venetian, *getto* signifies a foundry for artillery. As the site of such a foundry, a Venetian island was named Getto. Later when Jews were forced to live there because of persecution, the word became synonymous with cramped quarters populated by isolated people.

The term is also used allusively for a situation or environment characterized by isolation, inferior status, bias, restriction, etc.

GOOD SAMARITAN

A person who voluntarily helps others in distress. Also Samaritan.

The term is from the parable of the Good Samaritan in Luke (a book of the Bible) in which a Samaritan stops to help a man who has been injured and robbed, while others passed by. The word *Samaritan* refers to a resident of Samaria.

56. Can you think of a word with three consecutive double letters?

Chapter 13

Lexicographer, There Is a Fly in My Language!

What do the words *acme* and *acne* have in common, besides being next to each other in a dictionary? The word *acne* began its life as *acme*. As a result of a misreading, it took on a new spelling. If you think about it, acne does result in many acmes (high points) on our skin. The English language is chock-full of errors that have now become so entrenched that we are not even aware of them, our elementary school language teacher notwithstanding.

Next time you see someone misspelling the word *definitely* as definately don't snicker. As of this writing, Google shows some 23 million places on the Net where the word is spelled as *definately*, more than 10 percent of the times *definitely* occurs. Chances are the new spelling will find a way into the dictionary just as *miniscule* did for the original word *minuscule* because people thought the word had its origin in the prefix *mini-*.

It's usage that determines the flow of language. Let's see a few words that are in their current incarnations because someone misread, misprinted, misheard, or misunderstood the term.

INTERNECINE
Relating to conflict within a group or nation; mutually destructive.

The original meaning of *internecine* was "deadly," from the prefix *inter-* (all the way to, completely) + Latin *necare* (to kill), from *nec-* (death). While writing his 1755 dictionary, the great lexicographer Samuel Johnson erroneously believed the prefix *inter-* implied "between" (as in "international") and defined *internecine* as "endeavoring mutual destruction" and that, thanks to the popularity of his dictionary, became the primary sense of the word.

Johnson wasn't shy from admitting an error, though. When a reader confronted him on why he defined the word *pastern* as "the knee of an horse" (instead of the part between the fetlock and the hoof) his reply was, "Ignorance, madam, pure ignorance."

Johnson defined a lexicographer as a "harmless drudge," but he had much to teach us. It'd be refreshing to hear that candid admission of error from today's political and corporate leaders.

DERRING-DO

Daring acts, often tinged with recklessness.

It's only someone like Samuel Johnson who can claim to change the meaning of a word singlehandedly. Usually, it takes many pens to shape the word gradually into a new form. The story of derring-do is something like that.

The *Oxford English Dictionary* shows the first printed citation for the term from Geoffrey Chaucer's *Troylus* published around 1374. Chaucer used the construction *dorrying do* meaning "daring to do." Monk and poet John Lydgate, an admirer of Chaucer, used the term in such a way that made it prone to be taken as a noun. In Lydgate's later edition the term was misprinted as "derrynge do." Poet Edmund Spenser began using it as a noun, and finally its appearance in Sir Walter Scott's *Ivanhoe* reinforced the new spelling and new meaning.

FAINEANT

Idle; also, an idler, a do-nothing.

The history of *faineant* is the story of how a feigner became an idler. The original word was French *faignant* (feigning). The word sounded to many listeners as *fait-néant* (literally, "does nothing"), and eventually it morphed into *faineant*. But then "feigning" and "doing nothing" aren't much different when it comes to shirking from work.

The French found the word useful and even turned it into a verb: *faineanter* (to laze about). In French history, many kings have been called *les rois fainéants* as the real power was in the hands of the mayors of the palace. Some could be deemed victims of the historiographers' biases, but there were some real do-nothings, especially the last kings in the Merovingian dynasty (476–750). Those child kings were symbolic figures at best, mere puppets in the hands of the officials.

SAND-BLIND

Partially blind.

The original word was *samblind*, from Old English prefix *sam-*, meaning "half." In a process known as folk etymology, the similar sounds of *sam* and *sand* resulted in an erroneous belief that the term referred to blindness caused by sand, and the word transformed into *sand-blind*. Sam Johnson is perhaps equally to blame here for defining the term as "having a defect in the eyes, by which small particles appear to fly before them."

In Shakespeare's *Merchant of Venice*, on his father Gobbo's inability to recognize him, Launcelot says:

57. What's the longest word found in Shakespeare's works?

O heavens, this is my true-begotten father!
who, being more than sand-blind, high-gravel blind,
knows me not.

The Old English prefix *sam-* is derived from the same root as the prefixes Latin *semi-*, Greek *hemi-*, and Latin *sesqui-* (one and a half), as in sesquicentennial (150th anniversary), but not French *demi-*. A coinage that enthusiastically employs many of these in a single word is hemidemisemiquaver (see page 100).

If *sand-blind* got a spelling makeover, here is another word that got an inside makeover: *purblind*. Originally it meant pure blind or completely blind; today it means partially blind.

False Splitting

Q: *What do a newt, a nickname, an uncle, an apron, and an adder have in common?*

A: *Earlier, these words were:* an ewte, an ekename, a nuncle, a napperon, *and* a nadder.

Read those two sentences aloud and you can see what's going on. The indefinite article *a* or *an* is getting sandwiched to the following word and then the result is being chopped in the wrong place. Linguists call this misdivision metanalysis. It sounds so odd today that a word might change just like that. Remember, the printing press was invented just a few hundred years ago. Before that, language was strictly an oral (no, not *a noral*) business. People spelled phonetically. Even by his time,

58. *What's a synonym of the word* synonym?

Shakespeare spelled his name a number of ways (Shakespear, Shakspere, Shaxper, and so on).

So, one would hear "a noumpere" and take it as "an oumpere" and eventually *oumpere*, or *umpire*, took root. By the way, an *umpire* is, etymologically speaking, a *non peer*, one who is different from the players. The expression *mine aunt* has been found written as *my naunt* for quite a few centuries in the past.

The same false splitting gave birth to the word *nonce* (usually found in the phrase *for the nonce*). It came about from the misdivision of *for then ones* (*then* was a form of *the*).

If you really want to appreciate the chasm between what is said and what is understood, try this experiment. Say aloud the expressions in the left column and ask a friend to write down what he or she hears. Chances are you'll see written the expressions in the right column.

paper view	pay per view
isle of view	I love you
new sense	nuisance
that stuff	that's tough
grade a	gray day
hill areas	hilarious
alien nation	alienation
final front ear	final frontier

And that's how *asparagus* became known as *sparrow grass*.

Sometimes words changed because we mistakenly thought we had a plural on our hands and fashioned a singular from it. *Pease* was one single little round green piece of the legume. But the ending sounded suspiciously plural (the plural of *pease* was *peasen*; think ox/oxen), and we formed *pea*. Now the old nursery rhyme "Pease porridge hot, pease porridge cold" begins to make more sense. It was the same story with *cherise*, which became *cherry*. In French, a cherry is still called *une cerise*.

Sometimes a plural becomes so popular it ditches its long-time singular garb and gets a new one in its own image. *Phases* was at one time the plural of *phasis*, but then we formed a singular *phase* from *phases*, abandoning the poor *phasis*. *Phase* isn't unique in this. *Termites* was the plural of *termes*, but we back-formed a singular *termite* from the plural *termites*. Similarly *primates*, which was the plural of *primas*, gained a new singular *primate*, modeled after the plural. We also formed a new singular *syringe* from the plural *syringes*, never mind there was an existing singular, *syrinx*.

Ghost Words

You, I, and other speakers of languages make mistakes, and sometimes those errors become entrenched in the language. But there are times when dictionary editors themselves goof up. Realizing just how deeply labor-intensive work is on a dictionary, we'll not be too hard on them. And as Samuel Johnson once said, "Dictionaries are like watches: the worst is better than none, and the best cannot be expected to go quite true." Such mistakenly coined words are called ghost words. Here are some instances where dictionary makers introduced an erroneous word, accidentally, and sometimes even on purpose.

DORD

The word *density* had a short-lived synonym: *dord*. It sprang to life out of thin air, and when the dictionary publisher discovered it several years later, the word was sent packing.

In precomputer days, lexicographers used little three-by-five slips of paper to record words and their citations. While the second edition of *Webster's New International Dictionary* was under way, an editor received an entry "D or d," which was defined as *density*, where the uppercase *D* and the lowercase *d* were abbreviations for the word *density*. The editor conflated the letters as *dord* and a new word was born. In 1934 when the new edition of the dictionary came out, it had an entry for the word *dord*, duly defined as density.

About five years later, another editor discovered that there was no etymology for *dord* and investigated. The story came out and the word was excised. Lexicographer Philip Babcock Gove, editor-in-chief of the dictionary's third edition, shared the behind-the-scene story of *dord* in the 1954 issue of the journal *American Speech*:

> As soon as someone else entered the pronunciation, dord was given the slap on the back that sent breath into its being. Whether the etymologist ever got a chance to stifle it, there is no evidence. It simply has no etymology. Thereafter, only a proofreader had final opportunity at the word, but as the proof passed under his scrutiny he was at the moment not so alert and suspicious as usual.

After the single-line entry *dord* was removed, the empty space on the page had to be filled. What to do? The nearby entry *Dore furnace* was inflated from "A furnace for refining dore bullion" to "A furnace in which dore bullion is refined."

ESQUIVALIENCE

What is with the *second* edition of the dictionaries that they carry fake words, intentionally or unintentionally? While the

59. What's the word with the largest number of senses in the English language?

spurious entry for *dord* was an honest error in the second edition of *Webster's New International Dictionary*, the second edition of the *New Oxford American Dictionary* carried an intentional ghost word: *esquivalience*. This newly minted coinage was defined as "the willful avoidance of one's official responsibilities." The entry appeared complete with secondary senses, usage examples, and etymology, like any respectable dictionary entry.

The word about a spurious entry leaked, and the *New Yorker* magazine investigated. It turns out this creative word was born from the imagination of the editors of the dictionary—they added it to protect the copyright of their work. If other publishers copied the text from their book, they would copy that entry also, and it would be obvious where they got it.

Mapmakers often add a fictitious street as a copyright trap, and encyclopedia publishers are known to add a fictitious biography or two to their works.

We often criticize nonstandard spellings, *alot* in place of *a lot*, for instance, and nonstandard pronunciations, such as *nucular* for *nuclear*. But that's how the language has been growing all those years. After all *cannot* came from *can not*, and the current condensed pronunciation of *halfpenny* (HAYP-nee) came from the earlier distinct pronunciations of *half* and *penny*.

Ultimately, a living language is democratic—every time we write or speak we cast a vote for a particular usage. When it comes to language, it's best to vote with the majority or risk being perceived as uneducated.

60. What are you afflicted with if you have haplopia?

~ *Chapter 14* ~

Words About Words and Languages

"So difficult it is to show the various meanings and imperfections of words when we have nothing else but words to do it with," the English philosopher John Locke wrote three hundred years ago. Locke's words still ring true today. Just as it's hard for a barber to clip his own hair, a weighing scale to weigh itself, or a flower to know its own fragrance, it's difficult trying to describe a language using itself.

Fortunately, as an exception to shoemakers' children having no shoes, the English language has ample words to describe itself, its words, writing, speech, and other modes of expression. In this chapter we look at a few words about words and language. These metawords describe words and their arrangements, their precision and their imperfections, their use and their misuse. We could also call them word words.

LIPOGRAM

A piece of writing that avoids one or more letters of the alphabet.

In spite of what it sounds like, a *lipogram* is not a message with a kiss. It's a work written with a constraint. Imagine you've just begun your great epic novel and one of the keys on your keyboard is broken. It would be trivial to manage without a *Q*, *X*, or *Z*, but writing without a single *E*—ah, that'd be some challenge. If that sounds impossible, consider that whole books have been written without an *E*, the most frequently occurring letter in the English language. Without an *E*, one has to give up some of the most common pronouns such as *he*, *she*, *we*, *me*, and so on. What's more, even the article *the* is barred.

Coming back to books written without *E*s (I'm sure writing them is not something everyone can do with ease), Ernest Vincent Wright's 1939 novel *Gadsby* is written without the second vowel. One of the best known *E*-less works is Georges Perec's lipogrammatic French novel, *La Disparition* (The Disappearance). Its plot is full of wordplay, puzzles, and other word fun. For example, a character is missing eggs, or is unable to remember his name because it needs an *E* in the spelling.

Though it may be hard to believe considering the restriction under which it is written, Perec's novel is said to be quite engrossing. Apparently, many reviewers were not even aware that a special constraint had been used in writing it. After writing his book, Perec faced a protest from the *A*, *I*, *O*, and *U* keys on his keyboard that they had to do all the work, and *E* was leading an e'sy life. So he had no choice but to write a short work called *Les Revenentes*, where he put to work all those idle *E*s: the only vowel used was *E*.

If that doesn't sound incredible enough, here is more. *La Disparition* has been translated into English as *A Void* by Gilbert Adair. Amazingly, the translation also doesn't have any *E*s in it. In case you have not already noticed, both the phrases "*La Disparition*" and "*A Void*" have only vowels *A*, *I*, and *O* in them, the same as in the word *lipogram*. And *Void*'s protagonist is named Anton Vowl.

One can write numbers from zero, one, two, onwards, and not use the *A* key on the keyboard until reaching *thousand*. As for the literary merit of that composition, I'm not very certain.

Lipogram comes from Greek *lipo-* (lacking) and *gram* (something written).

HETEROGRAPHY

1. A spelling different from the one in current use.   2. Use of the same letter(s) to convey different sounds, for example, *gh* in *rough* and *ghost*.

The idea of heterography is a recent phenomenon, relatively speaking. Earlier, when English was mainly a spoken language, it was a free-for-all, spelling-wise. Any spelling was good as long as you could make yourself understood. Each writer spelled words in his own way, trying to spell them phonetically. Shakespeare spelled his own name in various ways (Shaxspear, Shakespear, and so on).

If you read old manuscripts, you can find different spellings of a word on the same page, and sometimes even in the same sentence. Spelling wasn't something sacrosanct: If a line was too long to fit, a typesetter might simply squeeze or expand the word by altering the spelling.

If the idea of to-each-one's-own spelling for the same word sounds bizarre, consider how we practice it even today, in the only place we can: in our names. Look around and you might find a Christina and a Cristina and a Kristina and many other permutations and combinations.

With the advent of printing in the fifteenth century, spelling began to become standardized. By the nineteenth century, most words had a single "official" spelling, as a consensus, not by the diktat of a committee.

Today if you write *definately* and someone points out that

61. What other country calls itself the United States?

you've misspelled the word, just tell them you're a practitioner of heterography.

The word is derived from Greek *hetero* (different) and *-graphy* (writing).

SPRACHGEFUHL

A feeling for language or a sensitivity for what is correct language.

If you have *Sprachgefuhl*, you have an ear for idiomatically appropriate language. The best illustration of Sprachgefuhl, or the lack of it, was an 1855 Portuguese-English phrase book intended to help Portuguese speakers master the English language.

The book, titled *English As She Is Spoke*, it was authored by one Pedro Carolino. The only problem was that Pedro didn't know any English. On the plus side, he did have a Portuguese-French phrase book. Pedro simply picked up a French-English dictionary and tried the circuitous route: Portuguese to French to English. The result was such gems as:

Names for body parts   "Of the Man: The inferior lip; The superior lip; The fat of the leg."
Food   "Eatings: Some black pudding; A little mine; Hog fat; Some wigs; Vegetables boiled to a pap."
Swimming instructions   "For to swim: I row upon the belly on the back and between two waters."
Idioms   "Idiotism: Cat scalded fear the cold water."

This book was even used as a textbook in the Portuguese colony of Macao. I regret to say they eventually stopped using

6.2. What's the only number that has as many letters in its spelling as its value?

it. Imagine, in just a few years, we could have witnessed a lovely new strain of the English language take root.

Pedro was simply ahead of his time. Today anyone can achieve the same results with computer translation.

The word is a borrowing from German *Sprachgefühl*, from *Sprache* (language) and *Gefühl* (feeling).

ANANYM

A name formed by reversing letters of another name, often used as a pseudonym.

Here are some examples of ananyms:

- Talk show host Oprah's production company is named Harpo.
- Doctor Seuss (Theodore Geisel) wrote many books under the name Theo LeSieg.
- English author John Collard used the pseudonym Dralloc.
- Samuel Butler wrote a satirical novel *Erewhon* (near reverse of *Nowhere*).

Ananyms are a great way to come up with a pseudonym, often used in literature and in real life to form names. The opposite of pseudonym is autonym, a person's real name.

The word ananym is a combination of Greek *ana-* (back) and *-onym* (name).

NEOLOGIST

One who coins, uses, or introduces new words, or redefines old words in a language.

A language grows by infusion of new words. Anyone who has been on the Internet for more than a few days knows what a webmaster is. Yet only a few years ago if we came across a *webmaster*, we wouldn't know what that person did for a living. Perhaps he was showing giant spiders how to weave a world wide web.

There are many ways to coin words. You can make words out of thin air: googol, a word for a very large number (1 followed by 100 zeros) was coined by a nine-year-old boy. It was the inspiration behind the naming of the Google search engine.

You can redefine old words. The Google name, in turn, became genericized as a verb meaning to search for something, not necessarily on the Web. Coining words is easy. Getting them into a dictionary, now that's a topic for another time— see chapter 2, "Didn't You Just Make This Up?"

The word is derived from Greek *neo-* (new) and *logos* (word).

BACKRONYM

A word reinterpreted as an acronym.

In a backronym, an expansion is invented to treat an existing word as an acronym. An example is the PERL programming language whose name is now explained as an acronym of Practical Extraction and Report Language.

When naming, sometimes a suitable name is chosen and then an acronym is retrofitted on top of it: USA PATRIOT Act (Uniting and Strengthening America by Providing Appropriate Tools Required to Intercept and Obstruct Terrorism). The clunkiness of the expansion is a quick giveaway. How about forming a backronym for *ACRONYM* itself: A Contrived Result Of Nomenclature Yielding Mechanism?

Often, backronyms serve a useful purpose as mnemonics; for example, see the entry for the term Apgar Score in chapter 11.

Backronym is a compound of the words *back* and *acronym*.

GODWOTTERY

1. Affected use of archaic language.   2. Gardening marked by an affected and elaborate style.

Now here's a word with dual personality. Poet T. E. Brown unwittingly helped coin it when he wrote a poem describing his garden filled with all that came to his mind: grotto, pool, ferns, roses, fish, and more.

When he needed a word to rhyme with *rose plot*, he came up with *God wot!* He used *wot*, an archaic term that's a variant of *wit* (to know), to mean "God knows!" and it stood out among other contemporary words in the poem.

If you wish to create your own godwottery, we recommend: sundials, gnomes, fairies, plastic sculptures, fake rockery, pump-driven streams, and wrought-iron furniture. A pair of pink flamingos will round that out nicely.

The word is formed from the line "A garden is a lovesome thing, God wot!" in a poem by Thomas Edward Brown (1830–1897).

CHARACTONYM

A name of a fictional character that suggests the personality traits of that person; for example, Mrs. Malaprop in Richard Sheridan's first play, *The Rivals*, was known for misusing words with humorous results. Her name was derived from French *mal-* (bad) and *apropos* (fitting). For more examples, see chapter 6, "Fictional Characters Who Came Alive."

A related word is *aptronym*, a name that's especially suited to one's profession; for example, Sally Ride, the astronaut; Dr. Paine, the dentist; William Wordsworth, poet; Larry Speakes,

63. How many countries can you name that have one-syllable names? Hint: Three of them are in Europe.

spokesman for President Ronald Reagan; and Sara Blizzard, TV meteorologist. This idea of people's names reflecting their lives is also known as *nominative determinism.*

Charactonym is from English *character,* from Greek *charakter* (marking or engraving tool) + *-onym* (name).

ALLONYM

The name of a person, usually historical, adopted by an author as a pen name (as opposed to using a fictional pseudonym).

When one borrows the content of another's book, it's called plagiarism. But when merely an author's name is lifted, the term is *allonym.* Sometimes it's done for parody. When hired by someone to do so, it's known as ghostwriting.

An example of a work written under an allonym is *The Federalist,* also known as *The Federalist Papers.* This collection of eighty-five essays about the U.S. Constitution was written by Alexander Hamilton, John Jay, and James Madison in 1787–1788. They chose to write under the name Publius in honor of a Roman official for his role in setting up the Roman republic.

Some people believe that Shakespeare's works were written by various authors who used his allonym.

Writing a great novel might be a breeze, but choosing a pseudonym, that's not easy! You could simply call it your *pen name* or *byname.* If you wish to appear sophisticated, you might say it's your *nom de plume* or *nom de guerre.* If you reversed your own name to coin a nickname, it would be an *ananym.* But why

64. NRG is another way to write the word energy—the pronunciation of each letter conveys the word. Can you find a similar way to write the words to describe the following: a sea animal, an address for a king, one who has slipped away from prison, a tent for American Indians.

not take a walk in a library, browse the spines, and select an allonym?

The word originated from the combination of Greek *allo-* (other) and *–onym* (name).

GADZOOKERY

Use of archaic words or expressions; for example, *wight* (a human being), *prithee* (I pray thee), *ye* (you).

It's okay to use an archaic expression to bring out a certain effect if necessary, but their overuse leads to gadzookery. The word is coined from *gadzooks*, once used as a mild oath, which may have been an alteration of *God's hooks*, a reference to the nails of Christ's crucifixion.

Here is how a BBC reviewer described the works of the author Georgette Heyer: "She wanted to write more serious historical novels. Unfortunately the books she wrote outside her period have a tendency towards the gadzookery of Baroness Orczy."

EPIGRAM

A short witty saying, often in verse.

An epigram conveys more in just a few words than a whole book could. The poet Samuel Taylor Coleridge described an epigram as:

What is an epigram? A dwarfish whole;
Its body brevity, and wit its soul.

Here is one from Benjamin Franklin that truly demonstrates the power of a pithy epigram:

Little strokes
Fell great oaks.

The word comes to us from Greek *epigraphein* (to write, inscribe), from *epi-* (upon, after), and *graphein* (to write).

DYSPHEMISM

The substitution of a harsher, deprecating, or offensive term in place of a relatively neutral term.

Dysphemism and its antonym, *euphemism*, are often two sides of the same coin. A guerrilla in neutral language might be called a freedom fighter by some but a terrorist by others. Novelist and story writer Nathaniel Hawthorne summed it up well when he wrote, "Words—so innocent and powerless as they are, as standing in a dictionary, how potent for good and evil they become in the hands of one who knows how to combine them."

Philip French, writing in the *Guardian* (UK), gives illustrations of both words:

> *In 1945, shortly after the final victory over Japan, newsreels provided evidence of another holocaust, the bombing of Hiroshima and Nagasaki. The Holocaust (the dysphemism chosen by Jewish historians to replace the Nazis' ghastly euphemism, The Final Solution) and the Nuclear Holocaust the one in the past, the other in the future were to hang over the next half-century like a mushroom cloud.*

The word is from Greek *dys-* (bad) and *-pheme* (speech).

URTEXT

The original or earliest version of a text, such as a musical composition or literary work.

"Snd urtext b4 9 2nite." Even though it appears like a word from texting, a form of shorthand used in modern cell phone messaging, the word *urtext* has nothing to do with it. In fact, the term has been around much before cell-yell added to the urban pollution. It comes to us from German, with the prefix *ur-* (earliest or original);. for example, Ursprache = proto-language.

It's believed that Shakespeare's *Hamlet* was inspired by a

play written decades earlier. Now lost, this hypothetical play has been called the *Ur-Hamlet*. Much evidence points its authorship to the dramatist Thomas Kyd (1558–1594). Shakespeare's *Hamlet* was first printed in 1603.

Tack the handy prefix *ur-* onto everyday words and you can get many useful coinages, such as *ur-history, ur-source, ur-novelist*. But remember, *urgent* isn't a synonym for Adam.

Interestingly, Ur was also the name of an ancient Sumerian city in Mesopotamia (now Iraq). Since Ur was the home of many early civilizations, one could say Ur civilization was an ur-civilization.

EPISTROPHE

Repetition of a word or phrase at the end of successive clauses or sentences.

One of the best-known examples of epistrophe is Abraham Lincoln's description of democracy "of the people, by the people, for the people." A counterpart of epistrophe is anaphora, where the same word or phrase begins a number of sentences, as in these lines from the poem "To my Dear and Loving Husband," by Anne Bradstreet:

> If ever two were one, then surely we.
> If ever man were lov'd by wife, then thee;
> If ever wife was happy in a man,
> Compare me with ye women if you can.

Combine epistrophe and anaphora and you get symploce. Consider these words from Anne Lindbergh,

65. This South American country is named after Venice, the famous Italian city of canals. What is this country?

Perhaps this is the most important thing for me to take
    back from
beach-living: simply the memory that each cycle of the
    tide is valid,
each cycle of the wave is valid, each cycle of a relationship
    is valid.

Think about the resonance these rhetorical devices create.
No wonder they are often used in speeches and poetry to mag-
nificent effect. In Shaw's *Pygmalion*, Professor Higgins says of
Alfred Doolittle (Elizabeth's father):

> *This chap has a certain natural gift of rhetoric. Observe the
> rhythm of his native woodnotes wild. "I'm willing to tell you:
> I'm wanting to tell you: I'm waiting to tell you." Sentimental
> rhetoric!*

Epistrophe is derived from Greek *epi-* (upon) and *strophe*
(turning).

66. *What does* parliament *have in common with* watch *and*
exaltation?

~ *Chapter 15* ~

It's All a Myth

When you call your good-humored friend jovial, do you know you are comparing him to Jupiter (called Zeus by the Greeks), the supreme god in classical mythology? Also known as Jove, he is considered the source of joy and happiness. That's the reason astrologers proclaim jolliness, conviviality, and sociability as attributes of those born under the planet Jupiter. The stately beauty of Jupiter's sister and wife, Juno (Hera in Greek mythology), resulted in the term *Junoesque* to refer to a statuesque woman.

Mythologies—Greek, Roman, Phoenician, and others—are rich sources of metaphors about human nature. They are veritable soap operas, filled with stories of love, heroics, vengeance, punishment, desire, guilt, and more.

Here are a few words derived from mythologies that have become part of the English language.

HERCULEAN

Requiring or having great strength or courage.

Hercules (also Heracles/Herakles) was the greatest hero of the Greco-Roman mythology. He was one of Zeus's sons with a mortal woman. When Hercules was an infant, Zeus's jealous queen, Hera, sent a pair of snakes to kill him, but Baby Hercules strangled the snakes instead. That itself should have told Hera to sit quietly and accept that Hercules was no ordinary boy, but she had other plans. She induced a fit of madness into Hercules that made him kill his wife and children.

Hercules then visited the Oracle at Delphi, who suggested a series of impossibly difficult tasks as a penance. His mission, should he choose to accept it, would be to undertake a dozen projects (known as the twelve labors) that included, among others, slaying a series of ferocious animals: a lion, a multi-headed Hydra, and monstrous birds.

And he had to do some major cleaning as well. . . .

AUGEAN

Extremely difficult and unpleasant.

King Augeas in Greek mythology had an enormous herd of cattle, but he neglected to clean his stables for some thirty years. All that manure piled up over time, and Hercules was asked to clean it up as one of his twelve labors.

There were no giant Caterpillars at the time that Hercules could have used. So he did the next best thing: He diverted two rivers through the Augean stables to wash away all the years of accumulated compost. Today Hercules would receive a citation for dumping untreated sewage into the rivers.

The term *Augean* is often used metaphorically to refer to a cleanup of something that's exceedingly filthy or corrupt, such as a government department.

Cleaning the Augean stables wasn't exactly a walk through Disneyland, but lucky for Hercules, that muck didn't wash back into the stable over and over again.

SISYPHEAN

Endlessly laborious and futile.

Sisyphus, the king of Corinth, was one crafty fellow. He

even captured Thanatos, the god of death. When Thanatos came to claim him, he captured and chained Mr. Death. With Death itself locked away, all the dying stopped. It was a major scandal among the gods. Eventually Thanatos was released.

For his next trick, Sisyphus told his wife not to bury him after his death. When he died and reached the underworld, he complained to Hades, the ruler of the underworld, that his wife had neglected to perform the proper rites and he needed to go back and set the matter straight. He was let go, but once he was back home, he didn't want to return to the underworld. If only there were proper information sharing between the Department of Death and the Department of the Underworld.

For all this trickery, Sisyphus was condemned to roll a giant boulder up a steep hill. When the boulder reached the top of the hill, it would tumble down, and Sisyphus had to start all over again. Roll up, tumble down, repeat. After Sisyphus's eternal punishment, any endless, futile, task is called sisyphean.

All Sisyphus needed was a tip or two from King Gordius.

GORDIAN
Highly intricate; extremely difficult to solve.

In Greek mythology, King Gordius of Phrygia tied a knot that defied all who tried to untie it. An oracle prophesied that one who would undo this Gordian knot would rule Asia. Alexander the Great simply cut the knot with one stroke of his sword. Hence the saying, "To cut the Gordian knot," meaning to solve a difficult problem by a simple, bold, and effective action.

67. What's the longest word you can make using Roman numerals?

A magazine ad touts the efficiency of a product very forcefully. A graphic shows a classic maze scene complete with a guinea pig and a slice of carrot in one corner. In the traditional experiment, the little animal is supposed to find his way through the maze, backtracking, remembering the paths already taken, and ultimately reaching the reward. Instead, in this scene, the rodent zooms across the diagonal, turning the parts of the maze in his way to dust, and claiming the prize he richly deserves. That was a perfect illustration for the idiom *cutting the Gordian knot.*

Pandora sure could have used a Gordian knot or two around her box.

PANDORA'S BOX

A source of many unforeseen troubles.

We all know what curiosity did to the cat, but in Pandora's case it brought trouble to all humankind. In Greek mythology, the titan Epimetheus bestowed a quality to each animal. By the time it was man's turn there was nothing left. His brother Prometheus stole fire from Zeus and handed it to the humans, as he felt they ought to have the best gift of all.

That annoyed Zeus, king of the gods, so much that he chained Prometheus to a rock and had a vulture eat his liver every day. Since Prometheus was immortal, his liver grew back daily, but still he had to go through the torture. He was rescued by Hercules as part of his twelve labors.

To counteract the gift that Prometheus had given to humankind, Zeus ordered Hephaestus, the patron of craftsmen, to craft a woman out of clay, to whom various gods gave many

68. If you spell out numbers and write them in alphabetical order, what number will come last?

gifts: beauty, dexterity, charm, . . . and curiosity. The name *Pandora* is derived from Greek *pan-* (all) and *doron* (gift).

This first woman was sent to Epimetheus. Prometheus had warned his brother not to take any gifts sent by the gods, but Epimetheus didn't heed the warning and married her. Pandora came with a box that was filled with all the troubles. Epimetheus instructed her never to open it, but she couldn't contain her curiosity. One day she decided to take a peek in the forbidden box, unwittingly unleashing its contents on Earth.

If only Pandora hadn't given in to opening that tantalizing box.

TANTALIZE

To tease or torment by showing something desirable but keeping it out of reach.

The term is derived after Tantalus in Greek mythology. Tantalus was a king of Lydia, and he offended the gods in many ways. He revealed secrets of the heavens to humans; he stole nectar and ambrosia that he then offered to humans; and he offered his son's flesh to the gods for a feast.

For all his sins, Tantalus was condemned to stand chin deep in water in Hades. Branches laden with succulent fruits were spread just above him. Water receded when Tantalus reached down to quench his thirst. Tree branches moved away when he tried to eat the fruit.

Tantalus should be thankful it was only fruit that was hanging above his head.

SWORD OF DAMOCLES

A constant threat or an impending disaster.

Dionysius I (c. 432–367 BCE) was the tyrant ruler of Syracuse (not to be confused with the Greek god Dionysus, after whom he was named). Among his courtiers was Damocles who fawned over him. He gushed over the king's good fortune, his riches, his power, and his happiness. Damocles' fulsome flattery sickened the king so much that one day he decided to teach his servile courtier a lesson on how precarious good fortune can be. Dionysius offered to exchange places with Damocles for a day.

Next day, Damocles was treated to a lavish banquet. A sumptuous feast was served on the royal table and servants waited upon him. It was truly a life of luxury—except that Damocles was made to sit under a sword hanging from a single strand of hair.

Properly the sword should have been called the sword of Dionysius . . . but Dionysius wasn't cheated in the English language—there's a term named after him, too.

DIONYSIAN

1. Cruel.   2. Uninhibited, frenzied, or orgiastic.

The term *Dionysian* reminds us of the cruel king Dionysius I. He hung a sword over the head of one of his courtiers to show him the fickleness of fortune. Dionysius and his son were notorious for their cruelty and were also called the tyrants of Syracuse.

A second and more popular sense of the term refers to behavior that's unrestrained and uninhibited. This sense arose after Dionysus, the Greek god of wine and fertility of nature. Dionysus was a son of Zeus with a mortal woman, Semele. When Semele was pregnant with Dionysus, jealous Hera planted doubt in her mind about the divinity of Zeus. Accordingly, Semele insisted that Zeus show her his true form. Zeus tried to dissuade her, knowing that mortals cannot look at gods without perishing, but Semele didn't give up. Zeus agreed, Semele died, and Zeus rescued the baby Dionysus from the womb and planted him in his thigh whence Dionysus was born again.

Dionysus is associated with religious rites of wild and ecstatic nature, and so frenzied, unrestrained behavior is known as Dionysian. His Roman name was Bacchus, and accordingly a drunken revelry or orgy is called a bacchanalia.

A song sung in Dionysus's honor is called dithyramb, and by extension it's used for any wildly enthusiastic piece of writing or speech.

A Scripps Howard News Service article from April 14, 2006, describes Las Vegas's bid for a baseball team as follows: "Sin City, that den of Dionysian excess, is making another play to land a major-league baseball team."

One of Zeus's sons became a poster child for unrestrained revelry and merrymaking, and another of his sons was known for being diametrically opposite.

APOLLONIAN

Harmonious, well-balanced, disciplined, and calm.

Apollo was the god of prophecy, music, light, healing, medicine, poetry, and manly beauty. Talk about being overburdened. In spite of holding so many portfolios, Apollo was known for his calmness.

Nietzsche used the terms *Dionysian* and *Apollonian* to describe the opposite elements of the Greek tragedy.

Apollo is associated with reason, order, harmony, self-discipline, and other noble qualities, but he wasn't above using his powers for selfish purposes. When Daphne spurned his advances, he turned her into a laurel. Cassandra's rejection of his advances resulted in her getting cursed that no one would believe her prophecies.

69. What letter of the alphabet is the dog's letter?

CASSANDRA

One who prophesies disaster and whose warnings are unheeded.

The term is coined after Cassandra in Greek mythology, who received the gift of prophecy but was later cursed never to be believed. Cassandra was the daughter of the Trojan king Priam and Hecuba. Apollo, the god of light, who also controlled the fine arts, music, and eloquence, among others, granted her the ability to see the future. When she didn't return his love, however, he condemned her never to be believed. Among other things, Cassandra warned about the Trojan horse that the Greeks left as a gift, but her warning was ignored.

King Midas certainly needed a Cassandra to warn him of the gift of a golden touch.

MIDAS TOUCH

An uncanny ability to make money.

Midas was a Phrygian king and son of Gordius. One day, Silenus, the oldest of the satyrs, was drunk—not unusual for satyrs—and wandered into King Midas's garden. Midas took him in and treated him well for several days. Then he took the satyr back to Dionysus. Seeing his foster father back delighted Dionysus, and he offered Midas a wish.

Midas asked for the ability to turn anything into gold with his touch. Dionysus warned him of the foolishness of such a wish, but Midas's greed overtook his thinking and he was granted the wish.

Midas returned home delighted. He ordered his servants to bring him food and wine to celebrate, but as soon as he put his

70. *What's the longest word you can find that has its letters in reverse alphabetical order?*

fingers on a loaf of bread, it turned into a rock of gold. When he touched wine with his lips, it turned into liquid gold. Then Midas realized his foolhardiness.

When he hugged his daughter and she, too, turned into a golden statue, Midas begged Dionysus to take his gift back. Dionysus instructed him to rinse in the Pactolus River to wash away his Midas touch.

In reality, it was a curse for Midas, but ironically today the term *Midas touch* is used as a positive attribute; for example, it refers to business people who can make any enterprise immensely profitable and to sports players who can take any team to victory.

Even today, however, it's possible to find illustrations of the side effects of the legendary Midas touch. Often, lottery winners' lives are turned upside down after winning millions. They become drunk in their newfound riches, squander it on frivolous things, and end up being worse off than before.

In life, often one person's curse is another's boon. In the case of Midas, it was Croesus who really benefited from the Midas story.

CROESUS

Someone of great wealth.

The story of Croesus is where history intersects with legend. Croesus (c. 560–546 BCE) was the king of Lydia. He was fabulously wealthy. It's said that Croesus made his fortune in mining and in sifting gold through the waters of the Pactolus River, where King Midas washed away his scourge.

After his name we have the simile "rich as Croesus" to refer to someone fabulously rich. In modern times, we may find characters reminiscent of Croesus. An intriguing yardstick of wealth is how much money it would be worth one's time to stop and pick up from the street. According to the Bill Gates Wealth Index by Brad Templeton, it is $10,000 for Gates. In other words, the Microsoft man makes much more than ten grand in the few moments it would take for him to bend over and pick up that money from the road. Wonder when we are going to get Gates as a new eponym in the dictionaries. In the meantime, we will make do with Croesus.

GORGONIZE

To paralyze, petrify, or hypnotize.

After Gorgon, any of the three monstrous sisters Stheno, Euryale, and Medusa in Greek mythology, who had snakes for hair. They turned into stone anyone who looked into their eyes. Their hideous appearance also resulted in the metaphor Gorgon to describe an ugly woman.

Gorgon comes from Greek gorgos (terrible or dreadful).

Words Derived from the Names of Mythical Creatures

So many fantastic animals live on in legends and mythologies they would virtually fill a zoo. Because these creatures are myths, they're not bound by biological rules. Sometimes they're part human, part animal. They could have a human head and an animal body, or vice versa. They might have one eye or a hundred.

These permutations and combinations of body parts make it look as though the gods were playing a mix-and-match game of combining parts to make a composite. At times, it takes more than a single head to make one of these mythical animals.

Here is a look at the menagerie.

HALCYON

Tranquil; joyful; prosperous.

Halcyon was a mythical bird, identified with the kingfisher, that was said to breed around the winter solstice. It nested at sea and had the power to charm the wind and waves so that they became calm. The word is from Greek *halkyon* (kingfisher).

In Greek mythology, Alcyone was the daughter of Aeolus and wife of Ceyx. When Ceyx drowned in a shipwreck, she threw herself into the sea. Out of compassion, the gods transformed them into a pair of kingfishers. To protect their nest, the winds were forbidden to blow for a week before and after the winter solstice.

PHOENIX

1. A person or thing of unparalleled beauty or excellence.
2. A person or thing that has regenerated or rejuvenated after a great misfortune.

The word is derived after a fabulous bird of great beauty in Egyptian mythology. It lived to five hundred years and burned itself on a funeral pyre to be born again from the ashes.

CERBERUS

A powerful, hostile guard.

Cerberus (also Kerberos) was the three-headed dog that guarded the entrance to Hades, the infernal region in classical mythology. Ancient Greeks and Romans used to put a slice of cake in the hands of their dead to help pacify Cerberus on the way. This custom gave rise to the idiom "to give a sop to cerberus," meaning to give a gift to quiet a troublesome person.

An antigram is an anagram where the rearranged word or phrase has an opposite meaning, for example, united = untied, violence = nice love. What antigrams can you make of filled and funeral?

Cancerbero (from Spanish *can*, "dog") is one of the Spanish terms for a goalkeeper in *fútbol* (football). Kerberos is the name given to an authentication protocol for computer networks.

ARGUS

An alert and observant person; a watchful guardian.

After Argus, a giant with one hundred eyes, who was sent to watch over Io, a woman loved by Zeus in Greek mythology. He was later killed by Hermes, and after his death his eyes were transformed into the spots on a peacock's tail.

CYCLOPEAN

1. One-eyed;   2. Huge;   3. Formed with large, irregular stones closely fitted without the use of mortar.

Cyclops was a race of savage one-eyed giants in Greek mythology. The name is derived from Greek *kyklos* (circle) and *ops* (eye). Cyclopes forged thunderbolts for Zeus in return for their freedom. Cyclopean walls were attributed to them for their strength in building such massive walls.

MINOTAUR

Someone or something monstrous, especially one that devours.

In Greek mythology, Minotaur was a monster with a bull's head and a man's body. He was confined in a labyrinth designed by Daedalus; he devoured seven youths and seven maidens every year until Theseus killed him. The word is from Greek *Minotauros*, a combination of *Minos* (a king of Crete) and *tauros* (bull).

72. *What word becomes shorter when two letters are added to it?*

HYDRA

A persistent problem or one that is present on several fronts.

Hercules' second labor out of the twelve was to slay Hydra, a nine-headed monster. Hydra lived in a marsh near Lerna in Greece. As Hercules lopped off one of Hydra's heads, two more grew in its place. With a little help from Iolaus, Hercules cauterized each head as he severed it. Hydra's ninth head was indestructible, so Hercules dumped a huge boulder on top of it, a solution worthy of Alexander (of Gordian knot fame).

DRAGON'S TEETH

Seeds of discord. Usually used in the form "to sow dragon's teeth": to take an action that leads to future conflict.

In Greek mythology, the Phoenician prince Cadmus killed a dragon and sowed its teeth. From those teeth sprang an army of men who fought each other until only five were left.

* * *

Stories of gods and goddesses, whether in the Greek mythology or any other, are filled with qualities we find around us every day. Who knows whether gods made us by giving us their qualities or we made gods after ourselves? As the French philosopher Voltaire said, "If God created us in his own image, we have more than reciprocated."

~ *Chapter 16* ~

Ultimately We Are All Related: The Story of Indo-European

The word *guru* came to English from Sanskrit (via Hindi). The word *gravity* is from Old English. Two words from two different languages, two distinct cultures, two faraway places. What in the world could *guru* and *gravity* have in common?

The two words are cousins. They have a common ancestor. They both descended from a common language, unlikely as it seems. A guru is someone venerable, someone weighty. You might say a guru is someone who has gravitas.

About six thousand years ago, people in what is now Europe and Asia spoke a language that was the ancestor of many of our present-day languages. Linguists call that mama language Proto-Indo-European, or simply PIE. The languages that came from this mother tongue are part of the Indo-European language family. Half of the world's population today speaks one of the more than four hundred languages that belong to this family.

PIE speakers spread to various parts of the world. There was no postal service, no telephone, no e-mail, no instant messaging, so their language evolved in isolation. In turn, it grew into various clans: In one part, it became the Indic family, which sprouted Sanskrit and in turn Hindi, Bengali, Romany, and others. In another part, it came out as Latin, which again gave birth to French, Spanish, Romanian, and others. Another such language family is Germanic, where English, Swedish, Yiddish, and others belong.

People for many centuries have noticed the striking resemblances among words of various languages. The most famous announcement came from Sir William Jones, a jurist, Orientalist, and amateur philologist, who was based in India at the time. In a meeting of the Asiatick Society in Calcutta in 1786 he declared:

> The Sanskrit language, whatever be its antiquity, is of a wonderful structure; more perfect than the Greek, more copious than the Latin, and more exquisitely refined than either, yet bearing to both of them a stronger affinity, both in the roots of verbs and in the forms of grammar, than could possibly have been produced by accident; so strong, indeed, that no philologer could examine them all three, without believing them to have sprung from some common source, which, perhaps, no longer exists.

It seems impossible that a single language might change so much that it might turn into something as far apart as Sanskrit and French, but then look at what happened to English. Old English changed to modern English in just forty generations. Even though both are Englishes, they are as mutually incomprehensible as Spanish and French.

Today, English itself is branching out into many Englishes: there are American English, Australian English, Canadian English, Indian English, Singapore English, Caribbean English, South African English, New Zealand English, and even a relatively minority British English.

What came before Proto-Indo-European? There has to be a

parent of this language, but we don't know what it was. The picture becomes fuzzier the further back we go.

Here are some examples of word connections that illustrate how seemingly unrelated words are related. Such words that are derived from the same historical source are also known as doublets if in the same language (for example, English *royal* and *regal*) or cognates if in different languages (English *gravity* and Sanskrit *guru*).

HIBERNATION AND THE HIMALAYAS

Hibernate, to spend winter in a dormant state, and the name *Himalaya*, both originated in the Indo-European root *ghei-* (winter). The name Himalaya is from Sanskrit *himalaya*, from *him* (snow) and *alaya* (abode).

The Indo-European root *ghei-* (winter) is also the ancestor of words such as *chimera* (literally "a lamb that is one winter," or one year, old) and *hiemal* (relating to winter).

NARK AND PINCE-NEZ

A *nark* is a stool pigeon or informer. It's also used to describe an annoying person, as in this article from the *London Sun* about a soccer player: "He's a nark, complaining all the time." The word is derived from Romany *nak* (nose).

The term *pince-nez* (a pair of glasses held on the nose) is from French, and it literally means "it pinches the nose."

Ultimately, both words for nose are derived from Indo-European root *nas-* (nose) that's also the source of these other

---

73. English has borrowed many words from Japanese; for example, zen, bonsai, origami. Japanese, in turn, has borrowed from English: erebeta, wapuro, terebijon. Can you guess what they mean? Hint: In Japanese the L sound is pronounced as R.

words for nose: English *nose*, Hindi *nak*, Spanish *nariz*, and related words *nuzzle*, *nostril*, and *nasal*.

ODIUM AND ENNUI

Odium is hatred accompanied by contempt. The word came to English from Latin *odisse* (to hate).

Ennui is a feeling of listlessness or weariness from lack of interest, and this word found its way into English via Old French *enui* (displeasure).

Ultimately, both terms came from Indo-European root *od-* (to hate) that is also the source of the words *annoy* and *noisome*. How did we reach *annoy* from the root word *od-* when they don't look similar at all? The Latin phrase "*mihi in odio est*," meaning "I dislike" resulted in the verb *inodiare* (to make odious), which became *anoier* in French and *annoy* in English. And *noisome* is, basically, "annoy some," similar to *bothersome*, *cumbersome*, and others.

REPINE AND SUBPOENA

To repine is to feel discontent, to fret, to yearn for something. The word *repine* is from *re-* + Old English *pinian* (to suffer). *Subpoena*, the word for summoning before a court, is from Latin *sub poena* (under penalty), which were once the opening words of a writ summoning someone to the court.

Both terms are from Indo-European root *k(w)ei-* meaning to pay or to atone. This root is also the source of the words *pain*, *penal*, *punish*, *penalty*, and *impunity*.

> **74.** *I enter my PIN number in an ATM machine's LCD display. What am I doing wrong?*

REJOINDER AND YOGA

A *rejoinder* is a sharp reply or retort. It came to English from Latin via French. *Yoga* is the Indian philosophy and discipline for achieving tranquility and balance, and the word came to English from Sanskrit via Hindi.

The common theme in both the words is the joining, as both are derived from Indo-European root *yeug-* (to join), which is also the root of *yoke*, *junction*, *junta*, and *conjugal*.

What's the big connection? In *rejoinder*, one comes back to join the conversation, so to speak. In practicing *yoga*, the supreme purpose is to attain unity with the divine. *Junta* is a joining of people for a specific purpose, *yoke* is the joining of a pair of cattle, usually oxen.

FLETCHER AND PULMONARY

A *fletcher* is one who makes arrows; *pulmonary* relates to lungs. What's the common denominator of the two? It's the Indo-European root *pleu* (to flow), which also gave us *flow*, which also gave us *fly*, *float*, *fleet*, *pulmonary*, and *pluvial*. Pulmonary, meaning relating to lungs, comes from the idea of lungs being spongy sacs as floaters.

Other related words are *fledge* (to feather), which resulted in terms such as *fledgling* (literally, a bird that has just fledged) and *full-fledged* (literally, fully-feathered).

And that's the remarkable thing about language—how one word could diverge into so many different senses. That *pleu-* also gave us *plutocracy* (government by the wealthy), from the idea of overflowing riches.

FIRMAMENT AND DHARMA

Firmament is a fancy word for the sky. It's also described as the vault of heaven. *Dharma* is the Sanskrit word for duty, law, right behavior, or religion.

What do the two have in common? Both come from the Indo-European root *dher-* (to hold firmly or support), which is also the source of *firm*, *affirm*, *confirm*, *farm*, *fermata*, and *throne*.

Firmament could be described as the place that supports heavens. *Dharma* is the law that is firmly established. *Farm* was, in earlier times, a leased property that required fixed payment. *Fermata*, a sustained note, needs one to hold firm the piano key, for example. *Throne* is a seat that provides support.

Going from firmness to music, agriculture, law, royalty, and beyond . . . who could have guessed?

RECRUIT AND CRESCENDO

The words *recruit* and *crescendo* appear completely unrelated. What could a recruit have in common with crescendo? And what could they have in common with *creativity*, *cereal*, *concrete*, *increase*, and *decrease*, after all?

All of the common words mentioned earlier came from the Indo-European root *ker-* which meant "to grow." This root *ker-* grew into other words, and from those words came these words, like children of children of children. For example, the word *cereal* came from Ceres, the goddess of agriculture, known for the growth of the crops. Here is how other words relate to the idea of growing:

creativity   the idea of creating or growing something.
increase   to make greater.
recruit   grow the number of people in a group.
crescendo   increase in volume.
concrete   to grow together, harden.
decrease   *de* means *not*, so *not to increase*.

The languages are not so different from one another. Many of the words stay almost the same in many languages:

Hindi   *narangi*
Italian   *naranja*
Arabic   *naranj*
English   *orange* (earlier the word was *norange*: a *norange*
   became *an orange*!)

Just as humans came from a common parent and became white, black, Asian, American, Italian, and so on, the languages that we speak have a common origin.

Ultimately we are all related.

75. *What's the only state in the USA that has the whole USA in it?*

Chapter 17

These Sound Good—Let's Copy Them!

Languages borrow from one another all the time. We got *sangfroid* from French, and they took *le week-end* from us. And both languages are richer for it. *Sharing* might be a better word, but linguists prefer to call it "borrowing," even though the "borrowed" word never needs returning to its source language. Words borrowed this way are known as loanwords.

Another form of borrowing is loan translation. In loan translation, we don't take the word from another language; rather, we translate it literally, word for word. The best-known example of a loan translation is the word *superman*, a literal translation of German *Übermensch*.

There's nothing sinful about this borrowing and translating. That's one way languages grow and expand. Romans did it wholesale from the Greeks. Interestingly, the term *loan translation* itself is a loan translation of German *Lehnübersetzung*, from *Lehn-* (loan) and *Übersetzung* (translation). *Loanword* is also from German *Lehnwort*. A synonym of the term *loan translation* is *calque*, from French *calquer* (to trace or copy). Here are some loan translations from various languages.

As an aside, a *claque* is a group of people hired to applaud at a performance, from French *claquer* (to clap).

SUPERMAN

Übermensch was philosopher Friedrich Nietzsche's term for an ideal superior man, from German *über* (over, above, beyond, or superior) and *Mensch* (man). In 1903, when George Bernard Shaw needed an English equivalent, he came up with the word *superman*. Shaw could very well have translated the term as *overman* or *beyondman*, but he coined *superman*, and the term has stayed with us.

Imagine calling a superhero Overman!

FLEA MARKET

The English phrase flea market is a literal translation of French *marché aux puces*, "markets held on verminous streets." In French, a *puce* is a flea, but the French also like to call their loved one *puce*. A Frenchman might call his lover *ma puce*. And she might call him *mon chou* (my cabbage)! They have many other unusual terms of endearment, but that's a topic for another time. And it's not that unusual, either—in English we call them lovebirds or lovebugs.

RUNNING DOG

The term running dog, meaning a servile follower or a lackey, is a loan translation from Chinese. It comes from Chinese *zougou*, from *zou* (running) and *gou* (dog), apparently as an allusion to a dog running to follow his or her master's commands. This term was employed in Chinese Communist terminology to refer to someone who was considered subservient to counterrevolutionary interests.

76. *Why do we say double-u instead of double-v for w?*

PAPER TIGER

Here's another loan translation from Chinese. We use *paper tiger* for a person, group, or country that appears powerful but is actually weak. It's a literal translation of Chinese *zhi* (paper) and *laohu* (tiger). It came into English when Chairman Mao of China used the term to describe the United States. Ironically, the term was later used to refer to China and especially its economy.

WHISKEY

Whiskey is "water of life," etymologically speaking. The term is short for *whiskybae*, which is another spelling of *usquebaugh*, from Gaelic *uiscebeatha*, meaning "water of life." In Scotland and Ireland, whisky/whiskey is still called *usquebaugh*.

This is a loan translation from Latin *aqua vitae*, literally "water of life." A dry spirit from Scandinavia is called aquavit. Russian vodka is water, too, from Russian *voda* (water). Finally, there's firewater, a literal translation of Ojibwa (an Algonquin language) *ishkodewaaboo*.

CLOUD-CUCKOO-LAND

A *cloud-cuckoo-land* is an idealized imaginary place disconnected from reality. By extension, it can refer to any state of overoptimistic fantasy that's free of problems. The term is a loan translation of Greek *nephelokokkygia*, and it came from the play *The Birds*, by the Athenian comic dramatist Aristophanes. In this satire, Euelpides and Pisthetaerus, two Athenians who are tired of the state of affairs in their land, persuade birds to help them build an imaginary city between heaven and earth.

WORLD-WEARINESS

It's a loan translation of German *Weltschmerz*, which is from *Welt* (world) and *Schmerz* (pain). We have also borrowed the actual German term *Weltschmerz* as if we are not sure whether to go with the translation or the original.

World-weariness and *weltschmerz* both describe pessimism, apathy, or sadness felt at the difference between physical reality and the ideal state, but *weltschmerz* could be more sophisticated world-weariness.

ANTIBODY

The name of these Y-shaped proteins is a translation of German *Antikörper*. Sounds like a perfect moniker for a supervillain.

THOUGHT EXPERIMENT

Mark Twain once quipped, "Some German words are so long that they have a perspective." Thankfully, we don't combine the words when we perform a loan translation from German. If we did, we'd be calling German *Gedankenexperiment* in English as *thoughtexperiment*.

BEER GARDEN

The term is a loan translation from German *Biergarten*, though we borrowed another German garden as it is: *kindergarten*, from German *Kinder* (children) and *Garten* (garden).

SLICE-OF-LIFE

Slice-of-life is a loan translation of French *tranche de vie*. It was coined by the French dramatist Jean Jullien and is from French *trancher* (to cut) and *vie* (life).

WORLD VIEW

It's from German *Weltanschauung*. Not only have we done the loan translation of *Weltanschauung* into English (as "world view"), but we have also borrowed the original term *Weltanschauung* itself as well.

* * *

Other languages also get loan translations from English. The English word *skyscraper* was borrowed and translated into Spanish as *rascacielos* (literally "scrapes-sky"), French *gratte-ciel* ("scrapes-sky"), and German *Wolkenkratzer* ("cloud-scrape"). By the way, the original skyscrapers were not tall buildings in New York City. The term was first used for tall sails in a sailboat. Great structures were much further down the line. Before them, the term referred to high-standing horses, tall men, tall hats, a ball propelled high in the air, and even a tall tale.

77. *What words end in* shion, *other than* cushion *and* fashion?

Answers to Puzzles

1. Aleksei Maksimovich Peshkov, who took the name Maxim Gorky. Would his quotations be called maxims?

2. India. It has more English speakers than the populations of the United States and the UK combined. Source: David Crystal, *The Guardian*, November 19, 2004.

3. W, whose name is three syllables long. No wonder we often abbreviate it.

4. Norway, South Korea, Philippines, Greece, and Peru. Find anagrams of your favorite words at http://wordsmith.org/anagram

5. True. America, Australia, Antarctica, Asia, Africa, Europe.

6. They have exactly the same letters, though in different orders (they are anagrams).

7. Who knows? The first difficulty in trying to figure out the number is defining what a word is. (For example, should *tables* and *table* be counted as one word or two? How about tabling?) Depending on the definition, one could come up with any answer. As a reference, the *Oxford English Dictionary* has around a half million words. The Global Language Monitor, a linguistic consultancy, claimed that in March 2006 there were one million words in the language. Source: The *Independent* (London, UK), April 13, 2006.

8. All three words are plurals that turn into singular words (brass, bibless, needless) when an *s* is added. Other examples are *millionaires*, *timelines*, and *princes*.

9. Forty and one.

10. *Frillless* (without frill) is one possibility. Here's another: *crosssection*.

11. Both *cookbook* and *checkbook* are horizontally symmetrical: These words, if cut in two horizontally, would produce mirrored images. Hope that spurs you to keep your finances and your diet balanced.

12. *Uncopyrightable* (15 letters). Another equally long word is *dermatoglyphics* (skin patterns or the study of them).

13. *Inkstand* has "st" in the middle, "in" the beginning, "and" the ending.

14. Each of these words changes from being a one-syllable word to a three-syllable word by appending just one letter: rode=rodeo; are=area; came=cameo. Some other words with the same property are Rome=Romeo and crime=Crimea.

15. *Beijing.* Another place name with three dotted letters in a row is *Fiji*, while *Ajijic* (Mexico) and *Ujiji* (Tanzania) have four!

16. *Deeded.*

17. She simply said, "Eve." Adam could have introduced himself with an even longer palindrome: "Madam in Eden, I'm Adam."

18. *Underground* and *underfund*.

19. *Fo'c's'le* (a variant of forecastle). You can even make that four by adding a possessive; for example, *fo'c's'le's gun*, but let's not get carried away.

20. *Feedback; boldface.*

21. *Asthma.*

22. *Nauruan.* This word has the distinction of being the only nationality word that's a palindrome.

23. The name Cristóbal Colón is Spanish for Christopher Columbus.

24. In the days of manual typesetting, capital letters were kept in a box on the top of the cabinet, small letters in a lower case.

25. Both names have three consecutive letters—the only ones among more than two hundred countries.

26. The letter *Q*.

27. Curtail=cut; regulates=rules; splotch=spot; deceased=dead.

28. Equatorial Guinea. Its official languages are Spanish and French.

29. Legos were invented by a Danish carpenter, and the name is a blend of the Danish *leg godt*, which means "to play well."

30. The abbreviation WWW has nine syllables compared to its full form, World Wide Web, which has only three syllables. WWII (for World War II) is another example.

31. *Spendthrift.*

32. Vladimir Nabokov, author of *Lolita*.

33. Maine.

34. *Best* and *worst*. *To best* and *to worst* are synonyms of each other.

35. *Screeched*, *scratched*, and *stretched* (all nine letters) are a few possibilities.

36. *Rhythms* is good. *Strengths* is even stronger; if you turn it into strengthlessness, you have a sixteen-letter word that has only one vowel used repeatedly.

37. The word *bid* vertically reflective in lowercase while its uppercase version *BID* is horizontally reflective.

38. Malayalam, a language spoken in Kerala, a state in south India.

39. *State* in English, *états* (a plural) in French. (*United States* in French is *États-Unis*).

40. Here's one: "There are three TOOs in the English language." It doesn't make sense as written but is clear when spoken that there are *to*, *two*, and *too* in the English language. Then there are some puzzles that work better when spoken. For example: What word begins with a *T*, ends with a *T*, and is full of *T*? The answer is *teapot*.

41. *Brougham*, which has half its letters (*ugha*) silent. It's a word to describe a four-wheeled boxlike carriage, and it was named after Lord Brougham (1778–1868), an English statesman.

42. Montana ("mountain"), Nevada ("snow-capped"), Colorado ("red"), and Florida ("flowery").

43. *Sequoia*. Another equally short word with all five vowels is *eunomia* (the state of having good rule or laws that are well administered). *Eunomy* is another spelling of this word. Yet another is *eulogia* (eulogies; or blessing). Then there is *aerious* (airy), which is just as short and yet manages to have all five vowels in order. To add the sometime vowel Y, make it *aeriously*! *Ultrarevolutionaries* has all five vowels—exactly twice.

44. Vermont, from French *vert* (green) and *mont* (mountain). The name of the Canadian city Montréal is derived from *Mont Royal*, the name Cartier gave to the mountain in 1535.

45. They are anagrams of each other.

46. After the first letter of each word is removed, the sentence becomes: "How his old Russian hat rings laughter, laughter rings out!"

47. Spandex, a synthetic fiber invented by DuPont.

48. All three were once trademarks. Other examples are *thermos*, *kerosene*, *velcro*, and *tabloid*.

49. *You* and *ewe*. Another example of words with the same pronunciation and no letters in common is: *eye* and *I*.

50. Japan: former capital city Kyoto, AD 794–1868, present capital city Tokyo.

51. All three words use all eight fingers of the hand once and only once when typed on a standard keyboard. Other words with this property are *panelist*, *pleasing*, and *lifespan*.

52. Eleven + two = twelve + one. There are a few possibilities in Spanish, too: *dos + trece = tres + doce* (2 + 13 = 3 + 12) and *uno + catorce = cuatro + once* (1 + 14 = 4 + 11).

53. Croatia. The word *cravat* was named after Croatian mercenaries in the French army who wore such neckwear.

54. Here are some: *erroneousnesses* and *overnervousness* (15 letters), *unceremoniousness* (17 letters).

55. South Dakota, the capital is Pierre.

56. *Bookkeeper*. An assistant would beat this bookkeeper: *Sub-bookkeeper* has four consecutive double letters.

57. *Honorificabilitudinitatibus* (twenty-seven letters), which appears in *Love's Labour's Lost*. It could be defined as "with honor." Its spelling alternates consonants and vowels.

58. *Poecilonym*, from Greek *poecilo-* (many-colored or various). *Polyonym* is another synonym of *synonym*.

59. The word *set*, which occupies twenty-six pages in the *Oxford English Dictionary*.

60. Nothing. *Haplopia* is the word for normal vision. *Oxyopia* is the word for unusual sharpness of vision—the interesting thing about that word is that it manages to stuff five syllables into just seven letters.

61. Mexico. Full name: Estados Unidos Mexicanos.

62. *Four*.

63. France, Greece, Spain, and Chad.

64. NMNE (*anemone*, which in Greek means "daughter of the wind"), UR XLNC (*your excellency*), SKP (*escapee*), TP (*tepee*).

65. Venezuela. In the fifteenth century, European explorers visited the place and saw houses built on stilts on Lake Maracaibo. This reminded them of Venice, and they decided to call the place "Little Venice" or Venezuela.

66. All three are used as collective nouns for birds: a parliament of owls, a watch of nightingales, an exaltation of larks.

67. *Cimicic* (seven letters), which means relating to cimicic acid, a foul-smelling acid obtained from a kind of bug.

68. *Zero*, the only number to use the letter *z* in its spelling.

69. R. It was called *littera canina* in Latin, literally "dog's letter." People thought the trill of its pronunciation resembled the snarl of a dog. In Shakespeare's *Romeo and Juliet*, the nurse says to Romeo, "That's the dog's name. R is for the dog." Incidentally, in Spanish a dog is called *perro* (with a trilled *r*).

70. *Spoonfeed* (nine letters). Another is *trollied* (eight letters). *Wronged* and *sponged* (seven letters) have their letters in reverse alphabetical order without any being repeated.

71. *Filled* = ill-fed; *funeral* = real fun.

72. *Short.*

73. *Erebeta*: elevator; *wapuro*: word processor; *terebijon*: television. *Terebijon* is often shortened to *terebi*.

74. I'm guilty of redundancy. PIN is Personal Identification Number, ATM is Automated Teller Machine, and LCD is Liquid Crystal Display. You could say I'm afflicted with RAS syndrome (Redundant Acronym Syndrome syndrome).

75. Louisiana, which has the letters *USA* in it.

76. We use the Latin alphabet (also called the Roman alphabet), which didn't have any letter for the *w* sound. The *w* sound was closest to *v*, so it was represented by *vv*. Since *v* and *u* are interchangeable in Latin, sometimes it was written as *uu*. Eventually, calling it *double-u* became more common while in writing, *double-v* became the standard. In many languages it's still called *double-v*: Spanish *doble-v*, French *double-v*. This *u/v* and *w* connection can be seen in cognates such as *guarantee/warranty* and *suede/Swede*.

77. *Parishion* (a synonym of *parishioner*) is the only other word, and it's obsolete. The pattern *shion* doesn't occur that often in the English language, anywhere in the word, not just at the end. Besides *cushion* and *fashion*, *parishioner* is the only word where *shion* occurs anywhere.

Acknowledgments

My sincere* thanks to:

- All the linguaphiles who shared their love of words with me at Wordsmith.org
- David Cashion, my editor at Penguin
- Judith Hansen, my agent at Marly Rusoff & Associates
- Carolanne Reynolds, the Grammar Goddess, whose sharp eyes and keen ears weeded out numerous errors from the draft of this book; Eric Shackle, for making it more readable; and George Pajari, for his knack for digging out the right reference material
- Karna Mathre, whose cheerful notes motivated me to keep going; Roger Chapanis, whose gentle voice gave me a little nudge, just when I needed it; and Bill Simon for his words of encouragement
- My loving wife, Stuti, and our lovely daughter, Ananya
- My parents, Sri Om Nath Garg and Srimati Krishna Garg
- My Guru.

Also to the authors of countless books on words and languages from whom I have learned over the years, and especially to the editors of the *Oxford English Dictionary*, a true lex icon, and the *American Heritage Dictionary of Indo-European Roots*.

*According to a popular story, the word *sincere* came from Latin *sine* (without) and *cera* (wax). The story goes on to describe the ancient Rome where unscrupulous sculptors tried to hide the cracks and other imperfections in their work by rubbing wax over them. So others advertised their wares as "without wax" meaning genuine. It's a lovely story but it's not true. The word *sincere* is, instead, derived from Latin *sincerus* (whole, pure, genuine).

Index of Terms